DAISY BATES IN
THE DESERT

Julia Blackburn is the author of *Charles Waterton*, *The Emperor's Last Island*, *Daisy Bates in the Desert*, which was shortlisted for the Waterstones/Esquire/Volvo Non-Fiction Award, and *The Book of Colour*, which was shortlisted for the Orange Prize for Fiction. She lives in Suffolk with her two children.

BY JULIA BLACKBURN

Charles Waterton
The Emperor's Last Island
Daisy Bates in the Desert
The Book of Colour

Julia Blackburn

DAISY BATES IN THE DESERT

VINTAGE

Published by Vintage 1997

2 4 6 8 10 9 7 5 3 1

First published in Great Britain by
Martin Secker & Warburg Ltd, 1994

Vintage
Random House, 20 Vauxhall Bridge Road,
London SW1V 2SA

Random House Australia (Pty) Limited
20 Alfred Street, Milsons Point, Sydney
New South Wales 2061, Australia

Random House New Zealand Limited
18 Poland Road, Glenfield,
Auckland 10, New Zealand

Random House South Africa (Pty) Limited
Endulini, 5A Jubilee Road, Parktown 2193, South Africa

Random House UK Limited Reg. No. 954009

A CIP catalogue record for this book
is available from the British Library

ISBN 0 09 975221 2

Printed and bound in Great Britain by
Cox & Wyman, Reading, Berkshire

*In memory of my father,
Thomas Blackburn,
1916–77*

· *Acknowledgements* ·

I was able to consult the Bates Papers in the libraries of Canberra, Sydney and Adelaide, and to go on an expedition to Ooldea and the area around Head of Bight and the Nullarbor Plain, thanks to a travel grant from the Society of Authors and the kind help of the Australian Tourist Commission.

In Australia I am indebted to Rory Barnes, who has done a great deal of invaluable research for the book. I would also like to thank Alec Baldock at the Streaky Bay Museum, John and Francis Barnes, Wendy Borches, Maggie Brady, Tom Gara and in particular Vida Thompson in whose house Daisy Bates had stayed during the late 1940s. I am very grateful to Archie Barton, the co-ordinator of the Maralinga Tjarutja Community, which now owns the lands in the Ooldea region, and to Denis Brown, who was our guide when we went into the desert. All the people I had the pleasure of meeting at Yalata and Ooldea were kind and helpful, but it was Nellie Queama and Huwie Windlass who gave me the most vivid recollections of Daisy Bates.

I would also like to thank Gwylan Bell, Shona Crawford-Poole, Kiek Droogleever Fortuyn, Toby Eady, Max Eilenberg, Christopher Glass, Dan Frank, Dan Franklin, Joy Jeffries, Gudrun Reinke, Basil Saunders and Mary Siepmann. My husband Hein Bonger and our two children Martin and Natasha travelled on this journey with me.

Part One

· *One* ·

There was once a woman who lived in the desert. There had been no rain for a long time and her eyes were tired from the dazzling brightness of the sky above her, the red monotony of the sandhills that surrounded her like a vast ocean. She wanted something green to look at so she took the stalk of a cabbage and leant it against the smooth trunk of the acacia tree that stood near her tent. Then she sat and stared at it, her thoughts drifting in the heat of the day.

I wonder how long that cabbage stalk managed to keep its colour and did the woman ever laugh when she realised it was still there, a sentinel standing guard over her after everyone else had gone home. Or did she not feel there was anything to laugh at, sitting in the doorway of her tent and gazing out, mesmerised by a fragment of green?

She looks down on the softly breathing skin of the lizard that sometimes sits on her lap in the afternoon, basking and catching flies. She imagines the sound the rain will make when it does finally come, like the pattering of flies' feet on the canvas of her tent. The rain will break through the layer of metallic scum that covers the surface of the water in the tank that is almost empty. The rain will bring back the birds with their shining feathers; it will bring life back into the desert and then she will watch as groups of naked people again make their way towards her camp. She looks down at the cloth of her long skirt which used to have a dense blackness but has now been turned into a strange patchwork of dull dark greens. She sees herself as a child in Ireland running through fields of deep grass; herself as a young woman watching a coastline receding into the far distance; herself as an old woman, here in the desert.

· *Two* ·

There was once a woman who lived in the desert and her name was Daisy Bates. I have set out a series of photographs of her on the table in front of me, like playing cards in the opening sequence of a game of patience. I look at the movement from youth to an extreme old age and in spite of the camouflage of time it is not difficult to recognise the same defiant face and the same stiff-backed body.

The young woman has an ear-ring hanging from the small lobe of her right ear and she is staring out into a sideways distance with pale eyes. How old is she, twenty perhaps? In that case she has seventy-one more years of her life ahead of her, all that battling and hammering at the gates of people and circumstance still to come. I try to decide from the expression on her face if she is as wealthy as she later said she was, or as poor as it seems she might have been. Daisy Bates was a liar, of that I am sure, but the extent and the exact details of her lies remain a difficult territory for which no good maps have survived.

I make a jump through time and here I have my

subject in early middle age, at the mid-point in her life, just as I am now, with the past and the future in a state of delicate balance. She has white-gloved hands folded on a black-skirted lap, a high-collared white shirt, a black tie, a black turban of a hat that looks as if it could also be used as a tea-cosy, and terrible dark glasses with round owlish frames that make her appear sinister, frightening, fierce, dangerous, difficult in every way that a woman like her could be difficult. I think I can just see her eyes through the dimmed glass and it seems again as if she is staring away from the lens of the camera, but now there is something disdainful in her expression, as if she does not want to waste her time looking ahead when there are so many more important things to be seen in another direction.

I imagine that the next picture I have chosen was taken somewhere on the Nullarbor Plain, the no-tree plain of southern Australia; you can see it stretching out around her and behind her, a parking lot of featureless land disappearing into infinity without even the distraction of a little bush or the rise of a hill. Daisy Bates is sitting on a chair in the middle of this expanse, her back as stiff as ever, and I can't see any sign of her tent. A wooden tea-chest is on the ground quite close to her and a large but unidentifiable object with a sheet draped over it is a bit further away on her left; she might be in the process of moving her campsite and then these things would be some of her worldly goods, packed up and ready to go. She is wearing an elegant, unbuttoned, black and white striped jacket, with a soft hat of indistinct shape pulled down on her head, and she is looking sad and serious but rather beautiful. There is a white cloth spread out on her lap and on it is perched a human skull without the lower jaw. Perhaps this photograph was taken to illustrate her belief that the Aborigines were a doomed race who would soon all be dead and gone with no one but herself to care about them and witness their passing, but again there is no way of being sure; it could also be the skull of a white man or woman.

Finally here is Daisy Bates when she was nearing the end of her life, a woman in her late eighties with the skin of her neck slack and reptilian and the lines on her face cut so deep that her chin seems to be attached by a hinge like a ventriloquist's dummy, while the creases down her cheeks and across her forehead could surely be felt by hands lightly searching for them in the darkness. The photograph was taken by the English society photographer Douglas Glass. He was in Adelaide for a few days in 1948, waiting for the boat that would take him back to England, and he began to make inquiries about Mrs Bates. He had read her book, *The Passing of the Aborigines*, and he must have heard quite a lot about her because by then she had become something of a legend, particularly in that part of southern Australia. Everyone he asked said she was dead; died some years ago in hospital, died just recently at Streaky Bay, no, at Yuria Waters further along the coast. They said she was very sad, demented, misguided, good, brave, bad; natives all gone and left her – beggars and derelicts, drunks and syphilitics – natives still there, with her to the end, dreadful sorrow. Eventually he tracked her down and found her living in a little suburban bungalow just outside Adelaide and being looked after by a lady friend she didn't seem to like very much. She was apparently delighted to meet Mr Glass. She dressed herself up in her best suit, the one that had been made for her in Perth in 1905; she clasped her umbrella in one hand and her handbag in the other and she posed on the verandah, an aged empress on her throne. There were daisies growing in the garden and she picked a few of them and held them between finger and thumb, gazing thoughtfully at her own namesakes. She went inside her little room and sat down to pretend to be reading some of her papers with a magnifying glass, the light from the window shining through the white strands of her hair. She led Mr Glass outside into the scrap of garden and showed him how she could touch her toes, swing her arms like the blades of a windmill and how well she could skip, up, up, up. 'Look, Mr Glass! Look at me!' Mrs Bates at the age of eighty-nine skipping in a field of daisies, or at least next to a flower bed in which a clump of daisies are growing. She laughs and says, 'So, Mr Glass, you must send the photographs to the newspapers. That will show them that I am not dead yet and don't intend to be either, there is still so much to be done.'

I would imagine that Mrs Bates told Mr Glass all about her life, especially her life once she had found her direction and was living in the desert. Her voice was deep, soft and clear even when she was very old, and even when she was very old she presumed that any man who pleased her would love to hold her in his arms if only she would agree to being held. I imagine her talking and talking for hours without a pause; the monologue of an isolated person who allows the threads of private thoughts to surface in letters and conversations, even in conversations with strangers. But perhaps by now she is much too old to talk like that and instead she sits there on the verandah, drinking tea and smiling, providing only tiny and truncated snippets of information that drift in the air like smoke.

If I could dictate the words, turn my idea of her thoughts into my idea of her speech, then she would begin by saying, 'I was once very beautiful, Mr Glass, but now as you can see I am very old instead,' pausing to let him stare and smile at her with the tolerant intimacy of someone who will not be staying long, inviting him to undress her of the burden of her age. She does not tell him that every morning she still stands naked in front of a mirror and because the sandy blight has made her eyes so dim she again sees before her, shimmering in the glass, the pink and delicate apparition of a youthful body. She does not tell him, but she looks into his eyes and there for a fleeting moment she can see herself as she once was.

An old lady is talking to a young man, wanting to charm him, to impress him with the complex uniqueness of her story so that he can carry some of it away with him when he goes, help her to outlive herself. Here she is, speaking, and if she says more than maybe she ever did or could say in a real conversation, that is because I am allowing her to speak with her thoughts just as much as with her voice.

'I lived in the desert for almost thirty years,' she says. 'That explains why the lines on my face are cut so deep. Look, you can see how the sun has burnt dark patches on the skin of my hands, my face, my neck, in spite of the protection of gloves and hats with long veils. My eyes are so tired, Mr Glass, and sometimes in the early morning when I wake up I seem to open them into a storm of heat and dust.

'I was five years at Eucla, on the south coast by the high steep cliffs. That was not my first camp, but it was the place where I first felt that I had cut the few remaining ties that held me to my own world. In the spring I could listen to the whales singing to each other in their wonderful solemn voices. The sound carries quite far and mixes with the sound of the waves and the sound of the air being sucked through the long underground tunnels in the limestone; the land there is all hollow, a honeycomb under your feet. I wonder if you have ever heard whales singing, Mr Glass, or seen them thrashing about in the water, male and female dancing together.

'Then I was sixteen years at Ooldea, much further inland and more bleak, but so lovely in its way. Perched there in my little campsite, the edges of my tent weighted down with empty kerosene cans filled with sand to stop it from flapping off like some great bird – and it would have, you know, it would have flapped away when the strong south winds were blowing. Perched there, doing what I could, close to where the Trans-Australian Line cut across those quiet red sands, making a track that could be followed by the sparrows, the rabbits, the foxes, the cats and all the whites, low whites mostly, and it was because of them I needed a revolver, not because of the natives. Ooldea had always been an important place for the Aborigines, there was fresh sweet water to be found there all the year round even during the most severe droughts. Then the water was gone, or at least most of it was gone because the trains used so much, but still they went on coming, passing through just as they always had done. It was a crossroads and a meeting place for them and you had the sense that there was a huge crowd there at all times, the dead as well as the living, watching and talking together. I suppose that might explain why I stayed so long, I felt at home there.

'In my dreams, Mr Glass, I often find myself back on the Nullarbor Plain, pushing a wheelbarrow along a stony track with a kerosene can filled with water balanced on it, like poor old Sisyphus with his boulder, up and down every day and no one to help him. I dream there is a storm, a wind rushing through my tent, blowing open the metal trunk in which I kept my papers, snatching up a flurry of torn pages, used envelopes, the battered notebooks I stitched together, everything on which I had accumulated a record of my life; an important record of an important life. In my dream I run this way and that, trying to catch hold of a list of names, a description of an insect, a bird, a tree, the stories, the laws, the traditions of the people who became my friends and who called me Kabbarli, the Grandmother. I can still see the faces of the men, the women and the children who set up their camps close to mine and came to talk to me in their sing-song voices. Sometimes if I stare out at a far horizon it's as if I can just distinguish a new group of them coming towards me out of the red desert, shining and naked.

'I have kept some photographs of the Aborigines, but not many, they don't photograph well. This man with a white beard is my dear friend Joobaich, one of the last of the Bibbulman people from the Perth region, and this woman sitting in the sun surrounded by empty bottles and old tin cans is his niece Fanny Balbuk, a wonderful storyteller. I gave her the woollen hat she is wearing and I think I miss her more than anyone else I have ever known – I wonder if you can understand that, Mr Glass. And here is Binilya, a cloud woman from Tarcoola, with Dowie and Jinjabulla. If you look carefully you can see that they are blind. We sat together at a place near Eucla for almost three years but the time passed by so quickly. This is me holding my umbrella, my royal umbrella I call it, and each of the women standing around me had eaten at least one of her newborn babies. Cannibalism, but nobody was willing to believe me, not even when I had collected all the evidence.

'Look, Mr Glass, there's a picture of the train: great, black, noisy, metal thing – and you can see what the landscape is like, how bare. That cluster of buildings in the background is the station at Ooldea; nothing more than a platform and a wooden shed, and the noticeboard as well of course, telling you where it is that you are. I suppose it can hardly have changed in the years since I was there; I would love to go back and see it again once more.'

· *Three* ·

I first heard of Daisy Bates about twenty-five years ago when I was on the edge of my adult life: back straight, waist narrow, jaw always aching because I clenched my teeth in fear or perhaps in rage. I had established a curious friendship with a woman called Edith Young who seemed to me infinitely old. I suppose she was eighty or thereabouts, but I looked on her as a tangible ghost, a creature who had managed to defy time and death, probably because she talked so endlessly that she never gave either of them a chance to interrupt her. She lived in the attic rooms of a rather grand cultural institution, perched there like an owl in a tree at the top of three (or was it four?) flights of thickly carpeted stairs, and she was always busy writing the story of her life and painting watercolours of naked voluptuous ladies and thin naked men. Deafness and fading eyesight made her stand very close to whoever she was speaking to, her chin tilted upwards because she was so small and her grey eyes staring with the intensity of the almost-blind. She told me about books, lovers, war and the Blitz, orgasms, sunsets and Buddhism: a torrent of words that I was glad to accept as an explanation of what mattered in life. She had lived in Australia during the 1930s and when I asked her if she had enjoyed herself there she said in her funny shrill voice, 'Oh no, I *hated* Australia! I was so bored!' But then she went on to explain that it was not all wasted because she had learnt about Daisy Bates, the only interesting person with a white skin who had ever lived in the entire continent as far as she was concerned, and of Anglo-Irish descent just like herself. 'You must write a book about her,' she said, and although I had no idea then of writing anything about anybody, perhaps that is one of the reasons why I now find myself turning back to the story of a woman who lived in the desert, a woman who has inhabited a small corner of my mind for so long that it can sometimes seem as if I must have met her, but have simply forgotten the circumstances of our meeting.

There is another aspect of Daisy Bates I have carried around with me for many years. I once bought a photograph album in a London street market: a big book with black covers that was filled with unexpectedly beautiful pictures; some of them still clear and dark, others fading to a pale biscuit colour and in danger of vanishing altogether if they were left out in the sun. The album seems to chronicle a world tour made during the 1920s by four vaudeville artists, two men and two women whose names were Frankie, Heath, Osborne and Perryer. They visited Africa, India, Australia, New Zealand and Japan, and maybe other countries as well, although since they never captioned any of the pictures it is hard to be sure. It is as if the whole world has been jumbled together in this book, with continents and cultures running into each other as you turn the pages, and the only constant thread is the smiling faces of the four actors. They stand in a tight little group and smile while what must be the Niagara Falls crashes majestically behind them; they smile with their backs to a jungle, a mud hut, a religious procession. One of the ladies, dressed in checked gingham with a tasselled fringe around her knees and a flower in her hair, smiles as she holds the hand of a naked black child with the wonderful beehive domes of a Zulu village all around them. The other lady, dressed in a sensible gaberdine coat with a kirbigrip holding her bobbed hair in place, smiles as she rubs noses with a Maori in full ceremonial dress. Three of them stand and stare as a huge wave bursts against a sea wall defending a city without a name; two of them watch respectfully as clouds of steam belch out of a hot geyser in a country I could never recognise.

A little while ago I was looking at the pictures from Australia in this album. There is an entrance gate leading to some sort of government building; a grove of eucalyptus trees beside a lake and a bridge; a café called Petersons in a shabby town with a big steam train running through the middle of what seems to be the main street. On the next page the vaudeville artists take it in turns to stand on the bottom step of the opened carriage door of this same train, which has now left the civilisation of the town behind. They wave and look delighted in spite of the bleakness of the landscape all around them. Then there follows a collection of photographs of the Aborigines: a man with bare feet, dressed in thin and filthy clothes, a stick in his hand and an expression of terrible despair in his eyes, walking beside the railway line; a woman sitting in the dust, leaning against a table that has lost its top; another woman with short, blond, shaggy hair and a child clinging to her back, both of them blurred and ghostly because of a sudden twist of movement away from the camera; others, singly or in groups, men, women and children, all with the same expression of dazed sadness on their faces.

I have often paused over these images: the shabbiness of the clothes, the emptiness of the land, the almost warlike solidity of the train, but I only noticed recently that one of the little wooden buildings was called Ooldea, while another was called Wynbring, the names written in bold letters on white boards. With a jolt of surprise I realised that these photographs show the places that Daisy Bates knew so well, during that same time when she was camping close to the Trans-Australian railway line. So these battered remnants of humanity, drifting on bare feet among the dust and rubbish, are the people whose lives she wanted to share. I took a magnifying glass to scan the pale gradations of grey and brown, searching for what might be the outline of a tent or a windbreak or a woman dressed in a long skirt preoccupied with her work, but I could not find any traces.

· Four ·

How did she get there? From what point did she begin and what were the steps she followed that led to a tent in the desert, clinging on year after year like a person on a raft in the ocean, sometimes with hardly anyone coming to talk to her for months on end and not much to do except endure the heat and the isolation, keep notes, write letters?

A long time ago I visited an astrologer who examined the palm of my right hand. 'How interesting,' he said, 'that explains it. Do you see how this line is split in two? You must have changed the direction your life was going to take. I have only met it once before: a sailor who gave up the sea.' I look now at the underbelly of my own hand, the complicated scratch marks that I do not know how to interpret, and I wonder which line represents the life I did not take.

A history teacher when I was at school once took a pencil and pushed it, point first, through a clean sheet of paper. 'That is what our lives are like,' she said. 'The shortening end of the pencil is our future and the lengthening end is our past. We are here, at the intersection of the two.' It was an image of such finite clarity, so different from my own experience of being in the world, surrounded by a maze of little paths like the tracks made by some small foraging animal and always the sense of the vast landscape of time, with figures walking across it this way and that.

I sit quietly in a little room surrounded by some of the things I have accumulated over the years: books, pictures, letters, objects, each with a story attached to it and a hook that can pull me back towards a memory or an association until it dances before my eyes. There are many traces of Daisy Bates to be found here among all this personal driftwood; sometimes it seems as if she has taken up residence like a stray cat seeking shelter during the winter but ready to leave again as soon as the weather is fine. On my right the Aborigine with his digging stick, whose face must surely have been familiar to her, walks in the dust of the Nullarbor Plain and stares at me with baleful eyes. On the window ledge there is a triangular silver-grey stone and a little painting of the horizon on a calm sea and the two together remind me of thoughts about the desert, although I don't quite know why. Behind my back there is a black metal box that once belonged to my mother's sister who killed herself in a garden long before I was born, and on this box there is a set of glossy contact prints: the photographs taken by Douglas Glass in 1948 and sent to me a few weeks ago by his son, along with an excerpt from a diary saying how difficult it was to find Mrs Bates, nobody knowing where she might be living or even if she was still alive.

The table on which I work is heaped with books and papers which are all related to the one subject. I have a blue file for copies of letters she sent to friends, a red file for excerpts taken from her diaries and notebooks. Slowly

I have grown accustomed to reading the handwriting of this dead stranger: page after page of the same person's way of thinking stretching backwards and forwards across the years, through health and sickness, determination and despair. Sometimes the handwriting is neat and precise, running like stitchwork in carefully regulated lines, sometimes it is incredibly wild: a few tangled words on the torn back of an old envelope, querulous lists that make no clear sense, questions that are never answered, native words without a translation. Sitting in her tent at the Ooldea Siding, not so long before the outbreak of the Second World War, she writes:

> No permanent home – nardoo
> toothpaste, salt, baking soda, chalk, borax, Ina, Junbur
> Whirlwinds
> Telephones
> Booming noises
> Breakdown
> Winds and winds
> The dead days [or is it the dead dogs?] of the
> afternoon.

I am trying to piece together a picture of someone else's life and character, making her recognisable even when she contradicts herself, building up a sense of what pleased her and what angered her; the threads that pulled her in certain directions. At times I might catch myself off-guard and read one of her notebooks as if it was one of my own: undated, battered, a hurried record of the events and the feelings that seemed to be important on a particular day:

> The sun falling quickly.
> Suppose one had neither past nor future, that

one only lived in the immediate twenty-four
hours. Loneliness does not block one's thoughts
and one wishes it would.

$$Bank = 16$$
$$59 \text{ bags}$$
$$8$$
$$\overline{}$$
$$176 = TOTAL$$

The stump-tailed lizard is too slow for this district, all living things here must be quick in
movement because they have to be able to take
cover from their enemies. Think of the wind on
a clear day blowing across the *mulga*.

· *Five* ·

I have a very vivid recollection of my childhood. Maybe it is because the world that I inhabited – the flat dish of a world that is inhabited by children – seemed to me to be such a dangerous place that it was important to watch it carefully; to be prepared for any sudden shocks. I can now if I want to return to that past time with an almost hypnotic precision. I walk up steep stairs with the effort of having only recently learnt how to walk; I move along corridors that seem to be endless and into one room after another. Sometimes I pause to look at the way the light comes in through a window or shines out from under a closed door. People come and go; they talk and they remain silent and a fleeting expression is held motionless like a still photograph cut from a film.

I know that if I were to visit any of the houses that I carry in my mind then I would probably hardly recognise them; the shape of the rooms, the height of the ceilings, everything might be at odds with my expectation of how it should be. And the people whose voices I can seem to hear and whose faces I can seem to see so clearly might appear like strangers to me. Perhaps I would have to realise that I had rolled several years into one dense bundle, huddled a crowd of disparate events into a corner like sheep, superimposed old age onto a face that was still young or given one person the expression that belonged to another. Nevertheless in spite of such confusion I am sure that the things I can remember are all in their own way true; it is that certainty which steadies me like the trembling arrow of a compass.

But Daisy Bates told lies. I am beginning to think that she must even have told lies to herself when she sat on her own in the desert, searching through the storehouse of her memory. It is such a strange idea: to look back at one's childhood and to invent what can be seen there; to create a father, a mother, relatives and friends, a house and even a landscape that never existed beyond the boundaries of one person's imagination. It would seem that for her the past had no fixed shape or pattern; it was a crystal ball into which she would gaze and she was free to interpret whatever images she saw emerging out of the glimmering refractions of light and colour. One day the vision might be dim and vague and she can see nothing but a stone farmhouse on a hillside in the driving rain, but then on another day the mist has lifted and she can recognise a beautiful mansion growing out from the side of that same hill and she is running towards it, opening a door, walking in and finding herself at home.

It must have been exhilarating, like having complete control over the development of a dream, able to make it slow down so as to focus intensely on a passing detail, race forward, swerve, leap, go whichever way you choose to go and stop at the moment you have had enough. She takes a dress, a delicate sky-blue satin dress, and she puts it on, slips it cold like a new skin over her nakedness. She takes a house, a beautiful house, and she gives it to her grandmother and comes to live there as well. The house is built of big blocks of yellow stone with deep windows and doors wide enough for elephants and she places herself right at the top of the broad sweep of the main staircase. Standing there in her sky-blue dress she pulls in the sound of laughter, the smell of woodsmoke from the fireplace mixed with the sweet smell of tobacco from her father's pipe, the barking of dogs, a pool of sunlight on the floor. She can hear someone calling to her, a rich mellow voice, 'Daisy, do come down. Daisy, we are all waiting for you. Daisy, we are going out in the carriage, do come now or we'll be late.' Slowly she walks down the stairs, step by step, closer and closer to the hum of life below her, and she is almost there when the thread snaps and she is back in her little tent in the Australian desert with the wind, the silence and the heat.

Long ago I had a friend whose family life was very chaotic. Her stepfather would get violently drunk, her mother was swept helplessly along like a tiny bird in a storm and her brother, who might otherwise have helped her, ran off to live with a fat wild prostitute who rolled her eyes at strangers and called everyone 'sugar' in an extraordinary deep voice. My friend responded to all this by adopting respectability. She would rise to her feet and salute whenever a member of the royal family appeared on television and each day she emerged immaculate and prim from out of the shouts and screams of her mad household. When someone asked her what her brother was doing she said he had married a Scottish schoolteacher and had gone to live in Glasgow, and when I saw her confronted by the spectacle of her stepfather thrashing on the floor like a beached fish, she walked past him confidently, tut-tutting at the untidiness as if he was a crumpled rug or a chair that had been accidentally knocked over on its side.

Perhaps Daisy Bates was already busy inventing herself, her history and her memories when she was still a child and then she never got round to breaking the habit or noticing that it was not the usual way of interpreting the world. A child somewhere in Ireland talking to a gathering of invisible friends is slowly transformed into an old lady in the desert, still talking to people whom no one else can see. A child takes a leaf and calls it a golden plate, smiling as she pretends to eat a slice of cake made out of mud; an old lady also smiles, eating bread and jam and calling it a grand supper party, with herself as one of the many guests.

'Who are you, little girl?'

'Oh, I am a princess. This is not my real home. I was stolen by a witch and brought here but I am going to be collected soon and taken back to my shining palace.'

'Who are you, Mrs Bates?'

'I am Kabbarli, the white-skinned grandmother. I am the Great White Queen of the Never-Never and I have come from the Land of the Dead to help my people in their hour of need. I am also a lady from a very good family, you can see that immediately of course, hear it in my voice. Several important men have wanted to marry me including a bishop and an English lord, but my destiny has kept me here.'

When she is famous, although perhaps not quite as famous as she thinks she is, a number of people are keen to ask Daisy Bates about her early life and she tells them everything that comes to mind, the story changing and changing again according to her mood. She tells of the beauty of her mother, the kindness of her father whom she loved so passionately, the good breeding and generosity of her grandmother. She remembers her brothers and sisters, the silver, the portraits, the lace dresses, dancing and riding on horseback. She will never forget the particular pleasure of shaking hands with Queen Victoria one bright sunny day. She couldn't have been more than six years old. Her Majesty walked towards her along the path in the gardens of Balmoral Castle and she can see it all so clearly as if it happened only a few days ago. She was not afraid. She made a curtsey just as she had been taught to do and then she held out her hand to the Queen and the Queen shook it. She will never forget the way that the Queen smiled, so kind and so gentle, a face very much like the face of her grandmother.

According to Daisy Bates's own various accounts of herself she was born Daisy May O'Dwyer in 1863 or 1861 in the village of Ballichrine, north of Tipperary and not far from Dublin. Her family were Anglo-Irish Protestants and they had been rich until their money was lost in the Crash or perhaps during the Great Hunger. She had one or two brothers, one or two sisters; certainly she was the youngest child. Both her parents died shortly after she was born or perhaps it was only her mother who died while giving birth to her and her father, her wonderful father, brought her up, took her with him on his travels, read her the stories of Dickens and taught her how to dance and how to ride a horse. 'Hands and heels down, head and heart up,' he always used to say and she has never forgotten that advice. Sometimes her father died when she was five and then her grandmother looked after her. This grandmother's name was O'Dwyer Hunt; everyone throughout the region knew her well, of course they did, because of her fine house and because she was so generous to the poor. When the grandmother died and the young Daisy was still in her teens she was made a ward to the family of Sir George Outram and with them she spent several fascinating and educational years travelling through Europe. They stayed in Rome, Florence, Paris and Madrid – her father would drop in from time to time – but she was glad they never stayed in Germany, even then she had an instinctive dislike of the Germans. Or was it Sir James Hamilton's family who adopted her after her grandmother's death? She had called her son Arnold Hamilton in recollection of their early kindness to her, when they took her with them to Europe.

And so it goes on, with the deceptions so numerous and complicated that it must have been exhausting to try and keep hold of the strings of all the stories that flew around her head. Perhaps when she was a child she was shown a photograph of a little girl in a lace dress shaking hands with Queen Victoria and that was turned into her memory of an event that she could see taking place in a sunlit garden. Both the Outram and the Hamilton families were listed in *Burke's Peerage* and it could be that she went through that fat catalogue of aristocratic names and decided she would have them as her guardians. Neither of them had any Irish connections or had ever taken a young girl called Daisy May O'Dwyer into their care.

When a biography of Daisy Bates was being prepared in the late 1960s a researcher went to Ireland to try to piece together the jigsaw of her early life. It seems that there never was a village called Ballichrine north of Tipperary. There was a Ballygorten and a Ballychrine much further to the west. There were no traces of a family called O'Dwyer Hunt having lived anywhere near to Tipperary and the people in the area were sure that if there had been a grand lady in a grand house who was generous to the poor then she would not have been easily forgotten. Towards the end of the last century there was a record of a man called Denis Dwyer who lived in the village of Ballygorten and a Michael

Hunt was living in the townland of Ballychrine where he owned land registered as being worth £6. 10s. There were also three Hunt brothers, who had owned a grocery shop in the village of Roscrea but they were all bachelors. Daisy Bates had described a high mountain called Caraig, rising up behind her grandmother's house; there was a hill with that name in the area but it was not especially high. The land around Caraig was used for growing potatoes and corn; it was not the kind of landscape through which a young girl would have been seen galloping on a fine horse.

In the early 1980s another attempt was made to capture the facts of Daisy Bates's life and this time an Irish relative was discovered living in Dublin in a house full of mouldy paper. From what she said and from other scraps of information it appears that Daisy May O'Dwyer was the child of a poor Catholic family. Her mother died when she was young and her father was a terrible drunkard who deserted his young family and ran off to America with a new woman, but he died while his ship was crossing the Atlantic. Daisy was sent to an orphanage near Dublin and she attended a charity school where she was trained as a governess. She was pretty and clever and well read. She learnt how to dance and how to ride and at the age of eighteen she was employed as a family governess, but there was a scandal and the young man of the house committed suicide. Shortly afterwards she set out for Australia, travelling as a free migrant.

In a letter to a friend that she wrote not long before her death, she says, 'Oh I do wish that I had some photographs of myself when I was young, although I hated being photographed if the photographers were men, I disliked their touch on my shoulders and arms. As a small child I was untouchable by any person except my nurse.'

· Six ·

Daisy Bates tried to shut out so many of the facts of her own life. She had a milling crowd of things she did not want to think about trapped in the dark room she had made for them and there they were, scrabbling at the door and waiting for a chance to escape and swarm over her. She needed to be on guard at all times, but still certain memories might creep up close, taunting her like the devils in medieval paintings that scuttle across the ground and fill the air with the soft rattling of their wings. Not long ago I was looking at a birthday book that had belonged to her, a little book printed in the 1930s with a quotation from Shakespeare for each day of the year, and I realised that the page on which her son was born had been carefully torn out. I imagined her tearing it out, quietly preoccupied with the task and perhaps hardly aware of what she was doing. I imagined her scrunching the page in her hand and throwing it away; as if it were possible to get rid of a detail of one's own history so simply.

As an old lady she sits in her tent and surrounds herself

with a babble of stories about all the adventures she has had, all the important people she has known. Some of what she says is true but a great deal of it is not and it is such an odd process trying to separate the person who she was from the person she would have liked to be, pulling the two apart and untangling their embrace. The one thing I can be sure of is her appearance: she was always an elegant and well-dressed lady who wore the same hats, coats, belts and shirts, year after year from youth into old age. Someone who knew her quite well when she was staying in Adelaide in the early 1940s described the curious unease she felt when she opened a cupboard in a hotel bedroom and was confronted by a row of starched white shirts, a row of long skirts, a row of tight-waisted jackets, all of them immaculate and identical like the chorus line for a play.

According to Daisy Bates's own account of her early life she came to Australia in 1884 or even as late as 1885. She travelled first class on a ship called the *Almora*. The weather was rough but she enjoyed storms at sea and the food and wine were plentiful and delicious. On arriving at Townsville in North Queensland, she was at once swept into a social whirl by relatives and family friends who were eager to welcome and entertain her. These people were just like her own people, their houses were just like her own home, she was very happy. The Bishop of Queensland made her his ward; a descendant of the State Governor wanted to marry her; she stayed with the Whites, one of the wealthiest families in Australia – her father had once lent them some money long ago so they were only too glad to repay the kindness. She travelled down to New South Wales towards the end of 1884 and she got herself a job; not that she needed the money, but she enjoyed the challenge. In this pioneering land even a woman of her class could take on work without any loss of social status.

At this point a certain amount of truth emerges and walks hand in hand alongside the invention, the tracks made by Daisy Bates in her high-heeled boots, clearly distinguishable in spite of the criss-crossing of other tracks. She was employed as a governess by the Bates family, who lived at Nowra not far from Sydney. Mr Bates senior was dead and his two eldest sons managed the estate, which was probably nothing more grand than a simple homestead with a few cattle and a dry expanse of land. In January 1885 she agreed to marry the eldest son, Jack Bates. The marriage was not a happy one and she often wished that her father had been alive because he would have warned her against it. She had just inherited five thousand pounds from her grandmother and like a fool she gave all this money to Jack so that he could buy them a property in Queensland. He wandered off to finalise the deal and when he returned the money had all disappeared and there was nothing to show for it.

It seems like a strange cruelty to challenge all this: to lead a fragile old lady back into her past and to stop along the way saying, 'Look, here is how it really was, and here, and here!' tugging at things long since dead to prove what their living shape must have been and how they were connected one with another. According to the surviving fragments of evidence that can be pieced together, Daisy May O'Dwyer arrived in Australia in 1883. It was true that she was travelling on a ship called the *Almora* – her name appears on the passenger list – but although the sea might have been rough the food and wine were not plentiful for her since as a free migrant she had to prepare her own meals and no one would have bothered if she went hungry. She arrived in Townsville with nothing – no money, no contacts, no plans of where to go – and yet somehow she did manage to jump from one stepping stone to another, inventing herself as she went along. The stories she told about her childhood and youth began to take shape and slowly over the years she built up a circle of influential friends who enjoyed her company and welcomed her as a member of their clubs and societies. As a young woman she was witty and charming, well-read and softly spoken. She had a natural elegance and a natural intensity that made men stare when she came into a room. Someone who knew her when she was in her early twenties said that she could 'charm swans off a pond if she wanted to'. Others accused her of being too flirtatious and too fond of men. A recent article in an Australian newspaper reinterpreted the same thoughts more harshly by saying 'she intrigued and used any means at her disposal, including her sexuality, to find security in a world stacked against her'.

There is no record of what she did during her first year in Australia, but by the beginning of 1884 she had got herself a job as a governess on the Fanning Down Cattle Station in North Queensland. A young man who at that time called himself Edwin Henry Murrant was working as a stockman at the same station and the two of them were married by a Catholic priest in March 1884. Looking at the marriage certificate there can be no doubt that the woman must be Daisy Bates; her signature is unmistakable, her father's name is O'Dwyer, her mother's name is Hunt, she was born in Tipperary and she gives her age as twenty-one although by then she would have been twenty-four. The young man who became her husband has been identified as the same man who was known as Breaker Morant or simply The Breaker. On the certificate he describes himself as a gentleman born in Devon and says that he is also twenty-one although he was only nineteen at the time. A month after the wedding he was accused of stealing some pigs and a saddle and he spent a week in prison. Soon after his release the couple separated and apparently they never saw each other again.

Edwin Henry Murrant was the son of a workhouse keeper in Devon who changed his name to Harry Harbord Morant not long after he arrived in Australia, and then claimed to be the dispossessed son of an English admiral. Just like his wife he used to tell stories about the elegance and wealth he had been accustomed to during his childhood. He had learnt to ride to hounds at the age of eight and he was banished from England because of a scandal in high places: card debts, a love affair and something to do with his naval college, although no one with his name appears on the Navy List of the period. Just like his wife he had a good speaking voice, a good knowledge of literature and he was quickly accepted into Australian society. Just like his wife he was a skilled horse rider and he became famous as the best horse breaker in the entire continent. Just like his wife he was fond of poetry and especially the poetry of Byron and he wrote popular bush ballads about horses and women and the roving life. In every way the two must have made a well-matched pair and even now when they have both been turned into legendary figures they must have an equal weight. Maybe they taught each other the gentle art of creating a past that had never existed or maybe their bond was based on a recognition of shared skills. I like to imagine them walking hand in hand through the corridors of their ancestral houses. They could have gone to Balmoral together and then they could have both met Queen Victoria in the garden.

In January 1885, eleven months after they had separated, the woman whose name was Daisy May O'Dwyer was married to Jack Bates at Nowra in New South Wales. On this certificate she gives the same place of birth and the same parents, but she declares herself now to be a Protestant, still twenty-one years of age and still a spinster. If anyone had discovered her deception she would have been liable to several years' imprisonment on a charge of bigamy, but no one ever did and she never mentioned her first husband.

The Breaker travelled all over Australia and then in 1900 he enlisted to fight in the Boer War. In 1902 there was a complicated scandal and he was accused of murder, court-martialled and executed by a British firing squad in Cape Town. I suppose that Mrs Bates must have read about the final stage of his life; the story of his execution was in all the papers. I wonder did she stiffen and feel her heart racing when she heard the news that he had been shot, just at the time when she was about to begin her new life in the desert, or was she able to tell herself that she had forgotten all about him?

· *Seven* ·

I'll give her a dream from her childhood which is a
dream that I used to have when I was a child. She
can have forgotten all about it for a long time until the
night when it comes back to her, unchanged and exactly
as it had been before, ambushing her at the moment when
she was just entering sleep so that her body shudders like a
rabbit dying and her new husband wakes and stares at his
new wife in the darkness.

There is a rope, a thin cord that stretches between
the earth and the moon. She has to walk along it across
the immensity of the sky with an old man sitting on her
shoulders, his legs clasped like claws around her neck. She
walks and then she falls, the old man falling with her, and
it is as if the rope slices right through her although when
she has stopped falling she can again feel it, narrow under
the soles of her feet. And if she cries out because of the shock
of the dream, does the man whose name is Jack Bates know
how to comfort her?

She says she fell in love with him when she saw him

riding a wild horse in a ring. Several men had tried but had been thrown off and now this man took his turn: the thick dust, the froth of sweat, the crowd cheering and shouting, the horse struggling to shake off the man and the man clinging to its back as if there were teeth in his thighs, like a terrier dog with a rat. A woman watching, smiling perhaps, deciding that this horse breaker would be a good replacement for the other horse breaker.

She says she had no idea that he planned to ask her to marry him. They were out riding near a place called Nowra when Jack suggested they have a look at an old church, opening the door and walking up the aisle hand in hand in their dusty riding clothes. Jack had secretly made all the arrangements beforehand and the priest was waiting at the altar, ready to bless their union. The priest's wife and another stranger were called in to act as witnesses; no one else was there.

Is that true, or did she beg him to marry her, seduce him with her tears or challenge him to the battle of coupling with her, rolling him in her thin arms and calling him her only, her beloved horse breaker? Sometimes when reading the stories that Daisy Bates tells about the events in her life, the only thing to do is to test each one with litmus paper: blue for what might be a lie, pink for what might be the truth, or is it the other way round? I doubt the details of the marriage, but I trust the reasons for her falling in love and I also trust the story of the dead man in the tree, even though it is a strange story that could easily have been invented.

She says that not long after the wedding they were caught in a thunderstorm while they were out riding. Suddenly a jagged line of lightning struck a tree close to them, splitting it open as if it had been cleaved by a huge axe. Within the tree there was the skeleton of a man, a spear clasped in the white bones of his hand. He had been held there, buried within the hollow trunk, and now that he was released by the lightning he was briefly able to stand upright, as real as a ghost. The body wavers and falls to the ground in a heap of loose bones and for the woman it is as if she has had a vision of God, fear, time, the human race: everything packed into the moment when the lightning split the tree open and revealed the secret that it had been holding for so long. The body wavers and falls to the ground and her husband has seen something that is grotesque and comic. 'Bloody blacks,' he says. 'Bloody blacks don't even know how to bury their own dead properly.'

After two years of marriage Daisy Bates gave birth to a son, her only child. They called him Arnold Hamilton Bates, although many years later when he is old and he must be well into middle age, she insists on referring to him as William. She is reported to have muttered darkly something about the difficult birth and how Jack was very understanding, 'he never came near me after that'. I don't know if she was always a cold woman or if she simply didn't happen to like her own husband: his smell, his manner, the expression on his face when he was asleep. She seems to have despised him and he in return seems to have hated her; at least he spoke of her with hatred when many years later someone tracked him down to a hotel in Perth and asked him about his wife. She blamed him for losing his looks, losing her money, losing whatever strength of body or character he once had. She was only able to speak about him with affection after she had decided that he was dead, swept out of the world while still a young man, leaving her as a grieving widow who could look back quietly on the happy life they had spent together.

Even during the early years of their marriage they seemed

to avoid each other's company. He would go on cattle-droving expeditions while she and the child stayed with friends or in hotels and I have no idea where the money came from or who paid for what; whether they had fierce quarrels or an agreement to be polite and distant. I also don't know if she had affairs with other men or if she just played with the idea of passion and physical closeness. She often boasted about the many men who wanted to marry her, offering her their grand houses and their immense wealth as well as their love, but no written declarations from these men have survived.

When she was already old, living in her tent close to the railway line at Ooldea, her writing is filled with an emotion which I suppose could be called sensuality. It is as if everything around her: the streaked violent colours of the dawn, the wind, the night sky, even the silence of the desert, has taken on an almost human energy and is trying to woo her, to possess her, to flood her with desire. She writes many letters to her friend Mr William Hurst, a newspaper proprietor she has only met a couple of times, and she tells him about the world that she inhabits.

> I love the whisper of the wind in the *mulga*, I
> have five of them around my tent here. To see
> a whirlwind in the making and watch it rise and
> progress and extinguish itself is most exciting.
> You are never quite sure it won't reach its zenith,
> so to speak, at your tent . . . In some places the
> women believe it brings babies to them.
>
> If my nights are wakeful I can look out and
> watch the movement of the stars. There is an-
> other me that seems even closer to stars, moon,
> trees and wind and as soon as I lie down this
> other me comes out from the shell of the day

and whispers lovely things to the stars and the
wind.

I wonder if this other person ever came out of what she
calls the shell of the day, at night with men or with women;
I doubt it but I cannot be sure; just as she invented things
that never happened she could also destroy the evidence
of things that did. But I find the image of the shell so
oddly disturbing: a snail hooked out of the protection of
its house; a hermit crab making the terrible journey from
one deserted container to the next, the soft vulnerable tail
of its flesh briefly exposed.

Whatever her relationship might have been with Jack
or with anyone else she felt close to, she was certainly
very cold towards her son. She spent the first eight years
in his company, moving from one place to the next, and if
she mentions the child at all she seems to be embarrassed
by him; he was awkward, uneasy, difficult in one way or
another, too like his father, a mirror in which she did not
want her own reflection to be caught.

In 1894 she announced that she had to go to England.
She said she must find out about a possible inheritance
from a relative in Ireland; her doctor had ordered her to
go because she was suffering from what was called nostal-
gia and there was only one cure; her husband was breaking
her heart and she must stay away until he had sorted out
his muddled finances and had found her a suitable home
where she could be happy.

Sometimes she told people that she took the child
with her, but that was definitely not the case. Arnold
was sent to some sort of boarding school and Jack or
Jack's mother could visit him or look after him when
necessary. With almost no money and no one in England
who was expecting her arrival, she set out on a boat sailing

from Perth. When the sea was very rough she and another woman played games: sliding across the sloping wooden deck on metal trays while the captain, members of the crew and some of the passengers laughed and applauded. It was five years before she felt ready to return to Australia, which must have seemed a very long time in the life of the child she had left behind.

· *Eight* ·

She leaves Australia and after five years she comes back to Australia. She watches the coastline slip away until it is lost within the horizon and five years later she watches as it surfaces again out of the far distance. She packs her bags to go and she packs her bags to return.

As I write this I can see myself standing on the deck of a ship, staring at the sea, the sky, the land; the wind cold on my face and all three elements seeming to be made out of the same translucent grey mist; layers of mist shifting and moving. I am no longer sure what year it was or where I was going but I can remember the intensity of my exhilaration because as I stood there I really felt for a brief moment that it was possible to become another person just by the fact of departure. It was as if the person I had been was left behind on the shore; a tiny figure standing there all alone and waving a white handkerchief at the vast silhouette of the ship as it churned out across the water.

Daisy Bates says goodbye to her son and her husband and to herself as a wife and a mother. She can explain to people in England that she is recently widowed or that she has run away from an unhappy marriage; she might mention the fact of a child, but this will probably not be necessary.

Later, describing her adventures, she tells a strange story about what happened while she was crossing the Atlantic; a story that is unlikely to have any truth in it except on an allegorical level, a way of illustrating a complicated and partly concealed thought. One night as she was sleeping peacefully in her cabin the waves got higher and higher until they flooded in across the floor. A suitcase that must have been under her bunk was pulled out like a little boat and all its contents were tipped into the water, a flotsam and jetsam of clothes and personal possessions. This was where she kept her entire collection of family photographs; not pictures of her son or her husband, but of her Irish relatives: grandmothers and grandfathers, aunts and uncles, dear papa and dear mama, a favourite sister and a beloved brother, the living and the dead all no doubt festooned with jewellery or medals or any other necessary signs of wealth and status in the world. She woke up in the morning to see them lurching with the movement of the ship, soaked to their paper skins, wet and bloated like the bodies of the drowned. So there it was; the evidence of the past had been wiped out in a single night, the ancestors were made unrecognisable and could not now be saved, the only thing to do with them was to scatter them into the sea, like ashes.

She arrives in England and makes her way to London where she goes directly to the Arundel Hotel in the Strand, a very fine and expensive hotel that her father had visited regularly, an uncle as well. In the morning she makes an appointment with the manager of her family bank; he has not seen her for such a long time, not since she was a child. Unfortunately the money she was expecting has not come through. Then she is off to Ireland to visit friends and relatives. She is sad to learn of the death of her sister Marion or was it Marcia, only a few weeks previously, but what parties, what a pleasure to go galloping across the fields of her youth, dizzy with the smell of wet earth, dazzled by the sharp brightness of green leaves and grass so different in colour to the soft greens of the Australian bush. A cousin invites her to stay with him in his mansion: a vast crumbling house that has not been touched since she last saw it but has been held in a spiderweb of the past like that room where Miss Havisham sits and waits for the arrival of her bridegroom. She walks down corridors that seem to be endless and here again are the ancestors: hanging in golden frames on damp walls, peering through the dim light with unblinking eyes and surely recognising her as one of their own as she passes them by.

In Ireland she had hoped to inherit some money from a deceased aunt, but she was again disappointed and when she got back to London she was almost penniless. Luckily she met up with a relative by marriage: General Brownrigg-Brownrigg was his name and he was the brother of her sister's husband, such a kind man. He arranged for her to rent a room in a hotel not far from the British Museum, a place that only catered for distressed gentlewomen, about twenty ladies with perfect accents but very little family wealth. It was General Brownrigg-Brownrigg who introduced her to W. T. Stead, the proprietor and editor of the literary magazine the *Review of Reviews* and of a magazine called *Borderland* which explored the possibilities of communicating with the world beyond the grave.

Once again fact and fiction hold hands and walk side by side. The drowned photographs in the cabin, the ancestral corridors in Ireland, the family hotel, even the recently dead sister, are unlikely to have ever existed; but there was a man called W. T. Stead and Mrs Bates was employed by him to work in his office; although exactly what sort of work she did or how long she stayed there is hard to tell. Mr Stead had a wide circle of influential friends; politicians, writers, feminists and psychic mediums were all glad to come and talk to him. He was a determined advocate of women's rights and had been sent to prison when he tried to expose the scandal of child prostitution in London. He believed fervently in the idea of life after death and was in regular contact with someone called Julia who dictated a series of letters to him from the Other Side. He died on the *Titanic*, very bravely so it was said, and on the night before the iceberg hit the ship he had predicted the disaster in a dream in which he saw hundreds of cats fling themselves from the top windows of a high building. But all that is by the by. Mrs Bates worked for Mr Stead and many years later when the possibility of her ever having known him was in doubt, she produced two letters to prove that she was not lying. 'Dear Mrs Bates,' said the first one, dated 6 July 1895, 'Herewith your salary for two weeks. Do you think you would like to come to the enclosed? Yours W. T. Stead.' 'Dear Mrs Bates,' said the second one, dated 24 December 1895, 'Here is your Christmas box, which I suppose you will prefer in currency to a goose or turkey. Yours, W. T. Stead.' She had owned a book with his dedication on the first page but she had given it away; she had lost all the other personal papers from that time and once she left her job she had not kept in contact with the Stead family.

When she was back in Perth Mrs Bates gave a series of talks to the ladies of the Karrakkata Club in Perth. She told them all about the two happiest years of her life when she worked first as a tea lady and general dogsbody in the office and then, thanks to Mr Stead's help and encouragement, as an editor and journalist. She had become a good friend of the family and had been introduced to many fascinating people. She once interviewed Sir Cecil Rhodes and was not at all afraid of him although she found his heavy jaw very unattractive. She met Andrew Carnegie, Thomas Hardy, Rudyard Kipling, Rider Haggard, Sir Arthur Conan Doyle, William Gladstone and George Bernard Shaw. She was there in the Mortlake Cemetery when Lady Isabella Burton tried to make contact with her dead husband the explorer, although that was not a success since Sir Richard had no words of comfort to offer from the grave.

Many years later in 1926 she wrote four articles for the *Australasian* magazine in which she elaborated on her memories of this happy time. W. T. Stead had told her that she herself was a psychic and that was why he had asked her to work on *Borderland*, but she did not believe in such things and told him so. Really his interest was only scientific and it was terrible to see how people tried to deceive him with photographs of ectoplasm and fairies dressed in gauze, tried to make him believe he had seen a ghost or had seen someone's Double, walking silently along a street, the face fixed with a look of extreme sadness. When these articles were published Mr Stead's daughter wrote an angry letter to the magazine saying that as far as she knew no one called Mrs Bates had any connection with either of her father's magazines and had certainly not been a family friend and confidante. Mrs Bates was very sorry to hear that her honesty was being held in doubt. She wrote at once to the paper, 'I could not contribute as *fact* to the pages of the Australasian, what was not fact; the whole of my life was so novel to me that its details stand out most clearly . . . My name was then as now, Daisy M. Bates . . . I am sorry that the articles should have offended Miss Stead but I think she is offended in a spiritualistic sense. She must have been a child when I was on the staff . . .'

There is one story that she tells about this period in her life which might perhaps give a clue to what was happening. She says that while she was working at the office she befriended a young woman whom she refers to sometimes as Lady Mary and sometimes as Rosalie. She employed Lady Mary as 'staff', to help with typing, and paid her whatever she could manage from her own small income. Then one day she had to face the fact that this elegant, aristocratic and frail young creature was working as a prostitute. She would accompany wealthy men to hotels or to their grand country houses, pretending to be a fiancée or a newly wedded wife, and in return she would receive whatever gifts they decided to give her. Maybe this is the closest that Daisy Bates ever came to describing the life she needed to live at that time; the way she was able to survive from one year to the next.

She says there was some sort of quarrel at the office, after which she never spoke to Mr Stead again. She went to Norwich because she had been offered a job as a librarian for a firm called Jarrolds, but this firm has a very thorough record of its own past history and there is no mention of someone called Mrs Bates having been employed by them.

Then the parties, the wonderful parties began again. A horseman called Carrick O'Bryen Hoare asked her to marry him and she refused not because she was already twice married but because he could offer her so little financial security. She was a guest at the castle of another of her double-barrelled relatives, a cousin called John Turner-Turner, and there she met Richard Attwater, the owner of Ratfin Hall. He also wanted to marry her, of course he did, and then she would have become Daisy May Attwater, lying in a feather bed in Ratfin Hall.

Sitting in her tent at Ooldea she wrote a description of that place which could so easily have been hers if only she had wanted it. Green rain-washed lawns, ancient cloisters of pale stone, a labyrinth of rooms filled with cabinets filled with precious ornaments; shelves laden with Wedgwood bone china; servants hovering in the shadows, eager to emerge as soon as they were called for. The image overlaps with a picture of her childhood home in Ireland, until the rain is soaking into an ocean of bright grass that laps around the edges of a vast and intricate building, a palace through which the mind can wander at its leisure. She pauses to pick up a shimmering cut-glass bottle or to stare at the dull sheen of satin and the ruffle of white lace in the painted portrait of some fine lady or gentleman.

· Nine ·

What does she expect when she comes back after having been away so long? The boat judders and is still, ropes are tied, gates are opened. She walks slowly down the gangplank dressed in a pale grey suit; there is a little hat on her head, a little smile on her lips, her hands are clean and her fingernails are neatly manicured. Among the crowd of people gathered on the quay she can see a boy and a man who are waving at her; they seem to be shouting as well but she can't hear their voices. The boy is less tall than she had imagined he would be and she would never have recognised him were it not for the man standing next to him, clean-shaven now and thicker in his body but still unmistakably himself.

When they meet, the child and perhaps the man also running towards her where she stands waiting for them, does her scalp prickle with fear or with pleasure, a sense of returning to where she belongs or a wish to clamber back onto the ship, hiding in her cabin until it sails away, taking her wherever it might go?

As soon as the child's face is on a level with her own she realises that they are the same height; they share the same delicate build. His face is flushed and damp with sweat and now that he is close to her he is confused, afraid that his stutter will betray him. Pity the poor child who has been trying to become a man while his mother was away but now wishes that he was so small he could bury his face against her belly and she must lift him up if she wants to look at him closely. Pity him standing there, staring at a woman who greets him with a rush of words and grasps his shoulders with thin strong hands.

I wonder if her husband will attempt to kiss her, stepping forward with his arms held wide as if he planned to corner her like one of the wild complaining cattle he so often had to move from place to place? Does she succeed in avoiding his mouth with a quick turn of her head and more excited talk so that he suddenly wants to strike her and shake her little body until it becomes less stiff? Or does he catch her in his arms for an instant, surprised by the fragility of her shoulders, the softness of her skin, a sweet peppery smell?

Daisy Bates wonders if she has aged as much as her husband has aged during the intervening years; it has not seemed like such a long time until this moment. With his moustaches gone his uncertainty is much more clearly visible. Was it Isabella Burton who said that her husband's mouth betrayed him: the mouth of a servant beneath the nose, the eyes and the high forehead of an aristocrat, or was it someone else who made the observation?

Daisy Bates looks at the child who is her son and she can see herself reflected there, but he is a mirror in a harsh light in which all the imperfections are revealed. He threatens her, this child, he threatened her when he was a baby staring so blank and helpless at her and something in his expression has not changed and never will. Later, lying in her tent, she is often visited by the memory of this meeting; walking down the gangplank and seeing him there, seeing both of them there; two close strangers who wave at her hopelessly from within a jostling crowd. Sometimes when she is on the edge of sleep she has the sensation that her son is staring down at her like the moon staring in through the open canvas doorway; scrutinising the flickering of her eyelids, the strands of hair, the spreading lines of age; trying to steal something from her.

Daisy Bates does not speak her thoughts. She smiles and laughs and chatters. Many years later she wrote a fragmented account of this meeting, how 'dirty, unmothered, neglected, incongruous' the boy was, how 'aimless and lax' the man. It's odd that she did not destroy this single sheet of paper since she destroyed so much else when she made a big bonfire by the banks of the Murray River. Maybe she simply overlooked it in her rush to sort out the past, or she could have wanted to keep it, just in case she ever forgot how disappointed she had been by that meeting, just in case she ever tried to turn it into a thing of pleasure.

There on the dockside she beckons to an old priest who is moving cautiously through the crowd and he answers her greeting and comes towards her. 'This is Father Dean Martelli,' she says. 'He has spent many years with the Aborigines at a Trappist mission in the north. Did I write to tell you that the *Times* newspaper in London has asked me to write about the Aborigines; they must have seen one of my articles I suppose. The Father has been educating me while we were at sea; I told him about that skeleton we saw in the tree, Jack, and now I understand what it was, what its meaning was. I can explain it all if you want me to.'

I see her standing there on the quay, laughing, boasting and telling lies even now when she has only just arrived.

I see her carried forward on a wave of restless activity; bustling past the child and the man and sweeping out their existence so that all they can do is stare at her and at the storm she whips up around herself. There is no article to be written for *The Times*; no one is particularly interested in her opinion on anything or how she chooses to live her life, but still she presses on, cutting a path as best as she can through the complicated landscape that surrounds her and trying to ignore the clattering tin cans of her own past which drag along behind her as she goes.

Within a few weeks Arnold has been sent to live with a respectable family called Brewer, who it is hoped will teach him better manners and improve his education. Jack lingers for a while in her company; falls asleep over a bowl of soup at a supper party, drinks too much, shouts, goes up north to organise the next cattle-droving job. Daisy Bates gives a talk to the ladies of the Karrakkata Club and makes friends with Mr Hurst, the editor of the *Australasian*, who is very impressed to meet a lady journalist working for *The Times* and fascinated by her description of what it was like to work for Mr Stead. She is introduced to Mr Forrest, the Premier of the State of New South Wales, and to the Governor and several other notables and they are all struck by her charm and her determination. They promise to help in any way they can and will be glad to hear about her travels just as soon as she comes back from them.

Her first expedition is quite a simple one: a practice run. She will join Jack at a place called Cossack, about a thousand miles up the coast from Perth, and then the two of them will travel inland with a pony and trap, looking for a property they can buy with some of her family money which seems suddenly to have appeared from out of a bank deposit. When she has found a place that seems right she will call it Glen Carrick in memory of that fine horseman

Carrick O'Bryen Hoare who wanted to marry her. Years later she will explain that she was forced to sell this property in order to pay for more supplies of flour and jam, but there are no surviving records that can prove it ever existed.

She gets ready to leave. She buys herself a long skirt with a leather edge to it, blouses, ties, gloves, veils, well-made boots with little high heels, and she laughs when she is warned of the danger of mosquitoes and snakes, white men and black men, floods and droughts. She travels up the coast on board an old steamer, meets Jack as planned and together they rattle across the wild countryside through rain storms and lightning storms, swamps and deserts. She doesn't much like being with her husband and pretends later that she wasn't with him at all, but apart from that she seems to enjoy herself immensely. She keeps careful notes about everything she sees: a beetle, a turtle, a big red false sun that hangs in the sky facing the true sun, a flock of birds that sing all through the dark night and have vanished by the morning. With the aid of interpreters she arranges her first tentative meeting with some Aborigines. She is taken to see a wall of rock that is covered with a mass of paintings in red, white and black. Perhaps there are some of those strange wide-eyed creatures with haloes around their heads or animals with intestines like island labyrinths, or a dense forest of red hands. She says enigmatically that the paintings fill her with envy, although she does not pause to explain what she means by this. Is it the sense of a continuity between a far distant past and the present that makes her envious, or is it the simple fact of there being another way of living in the world, a way different to anything she has ever known?

She returns to Perth without Jack and somehow manages to persuade the old priest she met on the boat to allow her to accompany him and his bishop on an expedition to the mission house at Beagle Bay. He agrees in spite of the fact that there is a strict rule against women entering the mission and no white woman has ever been to the area before. A boat takes them as far as Broome on the north-west coast and then they travel by mule for several days over a flat and monotonous land where nothing seems to be alive. They reach the edge of a swamp thick with water lilies and noisy with the screeches of water birds and there by the shore they are confronted by the collection of half-broken huts and shelters that goes by the name of the Beagle Bay Mission.

Daisy Bates sleeps on a sack on the ground with her head resting on a seaweed pillow. She works with groups of Aboriginal women digging a vegetable plot; she teaches the children to sing 'Here We Go Round the Mulberry Bush'; she helps the monks repairing the walls and fences. An old Spanish priest presents her with a lettuce that he has boiled until there is nothing left but a blob of green slime on a white tin plate. She is chosen to accompany the Bishop and a priest on a difficult surveying expedition when they need to tramp for days in a sweltering heat, staggering over stony ground and wading through swamps that cling to their legs. At night the three of them sleep side by side on the ground between the wheels of their little waggon. Daisy Bates asks them if they enjoy sleeping with a woman.

One day she and the Bishop go on a long trek to a mission station that is sixty miles or more further up the coast. They have to walk across mud flats in the full heat of the sun; the caked salt glistens like shattered mirrors, their footsteps breaking through the delicate pattern of movement left behind by the feet of birds, reptiles and animals.

They reach their destination at two in the morning and she is shown to a corrugated-iron store-shed where there are some sacks for her to sleep on. She is woken at dawn by the soft sound of women's voices and opens her eyes to see a group of about thirty naked women who have crowded around her, staring at her and discussing her among themselves. She gets up from her bed and as she begins to dress herself they move closer so that they can stroke the skin of her neck and shoulders, feel her long hair, take her small hands in their own. They watch carefully as she laces up her corset, tightens her belt, fixes the studs on a white collar and eases on her high boots with a shoe horn; each boot with twenty-six hooks and eyes.

· Ten ·

In 1905 Daisy Bates set up her tent with the Aborigines on the Reserve at Maamba in the foothills of the Darling Ranges a few miles east from Perth. She had been given a government grant to study the language and customs of the people who had been brought here from the surrounding area and she stayed on the Reserve for two years.

It must have been a bleak place, with government shacks made out of wood and corrugated iron, occupied by people who had become refugees in their own land. And there she is, living close to this restless confusion, filling the pages of the first of her endless notebooks and learning a routine that will never leave her, not even after she has left the desert.

The light of the dawn is soaking in through the canvas of her tent. Looking up from where she lies she can see the delicate tracery of the tee trees that should provide some shelter from the wind. She is lying on what is called a stretcher bed, set along one side of the tent and on the other side she can see the metal box containing her supply of food and a trunk with clothes in it. Behind her head a trestle table stands across the open back flap and on it are piles of books, papers weighted down with stones, a typewriter, an awkward tower made up of three willow-pattern cups and their saucers and a mirror the size of a face with a supporting metal frame that can hold it at any angle. Special cloth pockets like the maternal pouches of some marsupial creature have been fitted all around the sides of the table: a pocket for scissors and a nail file, a pocket for needles and thread, a pocket for string, perhaps even a pocket for her revolver or is that kept hidden somewhere out of sight?

Underneath the table she can just distinguish the big portmanteau case in which the rest of her clothes are kept; enough, in theory at least, to last for an entire year: a heap of white gloves, a heap of white veils, stiff collars to give dignity to white shirts, black silk ties, dark woollen stockings, long skirts that make you feel as if you are striding through deep water when they pull their weight at your legs. She has several wide belts with a stretch-mark on the notch where the waist is clasped; a delicate waist even now when she is forty-two years old, a waist that has hardly changed its size since she started wearing long skirts, except when she was pregnant once many years ago.

She lies on the stretcher bed staring at her possessions. The front flap of the tent is tied back and she can see the trunk of an acacia tree on which she has fixed a row of nails; one for the drying-up cloth, one for the washing-up bowl, one for her towel. A packing case tipped on its side can be used as a dining table and as a cupboard for cooking pans, while another packing case, leaning against the trunk of a tree, makes a good chair. A small folding card table with a green baize top provides just enough room for the typewriter, although it is not very strong and trembles or even collapses when the keys are being hammered.

She lies on that stretcher bed, her hands resting calmly on her belly, her head raised slightly by a hard pillow, and I wonder if her hair is long or short and is it already streaked with grey? I imagine her twisting it into a loose bun at the back of her neck, but perhaps that is later when she is older; in the few photographs I have seen from this time her hair is always hidden by a hat. I see her there in her tent and she reminds me of the marble effigy of a dead wife who lies close to the wall in the church of this village where I now live. The woman's husband lies next to her with a thin hunting dog sleeping quietly under his feet, while she has a swaddled baby propped under hers, like a little chrysalis. On her face there is a look of serene indifference to everything she has ever known about the world she has deserted, and I imagine Daisy Bates smiling that same cold smile and sleeping in a similar nightgown: long and white with a ruffle of movement at the wrists and around the neck. But I might be wrong, perhaps she wraps herself up in a sheet and sleeps naked.

She dresses meticulously, of that I can be sure, with all the ritual of a religious ceremony as she clothes her body with layer upon layer, pulling, belting, fastening, tightening. I wonder if she begins the day with gloves and hat already in position, or is that only later when she is going to be seen? She cannot wear gloves when she is massaging the naked bodies of the sick and anyway I sometimes think the gloves are only used to impress strangers, especially white strangers who might be quick to condemn her because she is the woman who lives with the blacks.

I wonder if she ever prays, all on her own in the desert, moving her lips in silence or speaking in a whisper to a god hidden somewhere in the expanse of sky, yellow and violet in the soft light of the dawn, scarlet and purple in the evening. Does she pray and ask for strength for what she is trying to do or forgiveness for what she has already done, or does she lie there breathing in the silence, private and self-contained in the nest she has made for herself?

I would also like to know how long she spends in front of the mirror. It is said that she was proud of her beauty, so does that mean she stares at her own face until it stares back at her and she can examine it with careful appraisal: small sharp nose, strong down-turning mouth where the lines of age will be drawn so clearly, pale eyes not yet damaged by too much sunshine, dark eyebrows, good skin?

She walks out to her kitchen and after searching the white ashes for a few glowing embers she gets a fire started on which she can boil some water for tea. If this is the first day of many years to be spent living in the desert, then on this day she has fresh bread, eggs, bacon, butter and jam. Later she must often try to adjust to eating almost nothing, her body desiccated like a fruit that cannot drop from its tree, but for the moment she has plenty.

She gazes past the clustered shelter of trees and bushes that marks her campsite and out at a wide river valley. At this time of year when some rain has just fallen, there are wild flowers bright on the ground and the scattering of trees and bushes receding into the far distance are covered with a haze of pale green leaves. It is much less desolate here than the places she will learn to know later.

Most of the people living on the Reserve are old. Here is one old man, who is the last surviving member of the kangaroo totem and another who is a dingo from the Victoria Plains, a woman who is a fish from the Capel River area, a man who is a snake, a woman who is a species of water lily. Old men and old women, they sit outside the government huts wrapped up in old clothes held to their bodies by rope and pieces of string.

The last of the sea mullet totem is also here, singing

songs and crying day after day, crouched in a corner with his back turned to any passers-by. And here is Fanny Balbuk busy walking to the same places she has always walked to, angrily crossing the platforms and tracks of the Perth Railway Station which has been erected on top of a swamp where she used to come and gather food, wading through the deep mud in the company of other women she once knew well. She breaks down the fences of people's back gardens in the suburbs of the new city because they stand in the way of the track she is following and she hammers and screams at the gate of a government building, behind which, somewhere among the complexity of metal and concrete, her grandmother's grave is hidden.

While it is still early in the morning Daisy Bates brews a pot of tea over the camp fire and then she waits until, one by one or in little curious groups, the people who have been watching her from a distance move closer. When they are close enough she can offer them tea, sugar, flour, speaking to them in what she has already learnt of their language.

· *Eleven* ·

I once stayed briefly with some gypsies in southern Spain. They lived in caves carved out of the rock: a honeycomb of open doorways leading into rooms that smelt of darkness and cold stone.

A young woman who I suppose must have been as young as I was then came up to me in the sunlight with a naked sleeping baby in her arms. When I said how lovely her baby looked she handed him over to me, telling me that I must press him close to the beating of my heart and then he would not wake.

I stood there holding that little sleeping body and the woman said, 'You can have him if you like. Take him, he would be happier with you.'

I had no wish to take her baby away with me, but for a moment I did suddenly want to cling to him. Then I could have gone into a house cut out of the rock and sat there with that pulsating fig of life in my arms; sat there and listened and stared about me and I would have had a sense of belonging and nothing else would have mattered.

I returned the baby rather abruptly to the woman and the connection between us was broken. Even now, all these years later, I can remember clearly how desolate I felt, as if it was my own child I had decided to leave behind. I suppose if I had been someone more like Daisy Bates I might not have returned him. I might have said, 'I'll help you look after him but I won't take him away. I'll stay here with you and your people.'

Perhaps something like that happened when Daisy Bates decided to live in the desert. To give up one world and try another:

Part Two

· Twelve ·

I am Daisy Bates in the desert, stretched out on the floor
of my tent, surrounded by the intense heat and dryness that
has not let go for months, or is it years. It is much too hot
to move. I lie on my back, naked and wrapped in a white
sheet, my eyes closed, my mouth slightly open. I suppose
I must look like a corpse waiting patiently for its coffin.

I lie here still as a stone and my thoughts race in
all directions: backwards and forwards as if there was
no past and no present time, just a single exploding
moment in which everything is contained. As a child
I learnt how to amuse myself with thought. I could be
trapped in a dark room and still I was free to go wherever
I chose to go. I could stare into the darkness and watch as
intricate images floated to the surface, as bright and vivid as
sea creatures in the moment when they have been pulled out
of the water. Sometimes I was frightened by the intensity
of my own imagination but I have learnt to get used to it
now, to tame it in a way. As soon as I began to talk to the
people here I realised that they have a similar ability, but

more powerfully developed than mine, perhaps because I was always isolated while they always had each other. You can ask someone here to tell you about how the world was made and as he talks you can see that everything he describes is happening again before his eyes, just as it did when it first happened: hills and plains are taking shape, rocks are becoming solid, animals are arriving and establishing their homes. You ask about something that has happened within his lifetime and you can see that he is reliving it as he tells it: a crowd of moving pictures flickering past; noises, smells, colours. I have never much tried to tell the people about my thoughts, it's quieter if I simply join them in theirs.

As soon as the sun approaches the horizon and the heat is less fierce, I shall get up, wash my body in tepid water, do my exercises, get dressed. Then I shall be ready for the new day just as night is drawing in. My eyes are not very good because of sandy blight but I know how to make myself presentable in front of the mirror, staring close at a face that is almost lost in the mist. I brush my long hair twenty times and tie it back in a bun so that the nape of the neck is exposed. The nape of the neck has always seemed to me to be more naked than any other part of the body. I wear high collars to hide my nakedness. The Breaker used to hate my high collars, he said he married me for the pleasure of removing them.

This evening I am going to invite some friends to come and join me. I shall take a few photographs out of the tin box under the bed: Sir Francis and Lady Newgate if I can find them, Lord and Lady Forster, and maybe a couple more. I will prop them up on the table so that they seem to be gazing towards me and then we shall talk and talk for hours. I will not forget to listen as well, being silent with full thoughts as I call it.

However, before the sun sets there is still the interminable waiting in the heat to be endured. Sometimes when I lie like this I can just see in the far distance the sharp green of a hillside. I can also see my tent: a white triangle in a red land, hanging there like the moon in the sky. The pattering sound of flies' feet on the canvas always used to make me think that it must be raining, but I am not so easily deceived any more. If it did rain I would stretch myself out on the sand and feel the water soaking into my skin. Perhaps my skin would erupt with flowers, just like the desert.

I wish my people were here. They have been chased away again but they'll be back. Black faces staring into my eyes until they seem to be exploring the cavity of my head, examining my soul, if there is a soul to be found there. Black hands as dry and soft as paper, white hands moist and clinging. Black skin smelling sharp and pungent; white skin sweet, almost deathly. I have very white skin, the white skin of a lady.

I wonder if my life up until now has been happy or sad, it is hard to tell. I thought I was happy when I was on the Maamba Reserve but then I believed a great destiny was sweeping me forward. I was at Maamba for two years filling notebook after notebook with stories and myths and vocabularies, as if it were possible to contain the mystery of a whole people like that. I thought that once I had made enough notes then I would have an important book that would somehow save the people from annihilation and I would be their saviour. Two years at Maamba, two years at other reservations in the west of Australia, a year in Perth when I was supposed to be getting my book ready for publication, and always the government was smiling kindly upon me and paying my expenses. I did write a number of articles for the newspapers and for some learned magazines, but I had no academic training,

I didn't know how to make a book take shape. Then in 1910 I was asked by the government – that nice man Mr Forrest – if I would be willing to help a young English anthropologist called Radcliffe-Brown who had come over from Cambridge University to study the kinship systems of the Aborigines. Of course I said yes, I felt that this was recognition of my·work and the first step towards success.

I wonder why I hated Radcliffe-Brown, Professor Radcliffe-Brown as he now is, quite so much? When I think of him something like panic rises in my throat. I can see him standing before me, a circus ringmaster if ever there was one, with his black cloak, gold-topped cane and carnivorous smile. Nothing touched him and he had no need of comfort, I suppose that was it. Before setting out for Australia he had done some work with the Andaman Islanders and he showed me a photograph of an Andaman Island chieftain and his wife. The man handsome and naked with a shiny bald head and his penis resting against his thigh. His wife smaller and just as naked, the two of them smoking pipes and smiling, proud and disdainful, a king and a queen. And there was Radcliffe-Brown crouching next to them with a microphone in his hand, not in the least bit aware of how ridiculous he looked. When I was with him he would interview men and women who were dying and a look of vague irritation would pass over his face if they died before he had finished collecting the information he wanted.

When he arrived in Australia Radcliffe-Brown was short of time and money. I was filled with such enthusiasm for the whole project that I managed to persuade a friend of mine – a banker who wanted to marry me – to finance the expedition with the sum of one thousand pounds. It was my money, I could have lived from it, worked with it, I might even have some now, but I gave it all to him. I also gave him everything I had written about the Aborigines: the manuscript of my unfinished book, notes, articles, everything. He wanted to interview as many tribal groups as possible within a few months, so I arranged to take him to a reserve over on the west coast near Broome, where I knew a traditional corroboree was being held, bringing together tribes from a wide area. We had only been there for a day or two when a mob of policemen raided the camp in search of a suspected murderer, so they said, and all the tribes scattered back into the landscape. It was then that someone had the idea of going to the 'hospital islands' of Bernier and Dorré where a number of different groups could also be found, neatly collected and held in one place.

In 1905 a group of government officials had decided that, because disease, and particularly venereal disease, was spreading so fast among the Aborigines, it would be a sensible idea for the men, women and children who were infected to be fished up out of the hundreds of thousands of square miles of the continent and taken to a place where they could possibly be cured and certainly could be prevented from spreading their contagion any further. So the sick and the dying were selected and herded into little groups, connected together in batches with chains around their necks. After a long journey from the forests, the deserts, the bush, the edges of new cities, they were brought to the port of Carnarvan and loaded onto a boat that would take them on the final stage of their journey: Bernier for the men, Dorré for the women and children.

On Bernier a wooden building had been erected at the highest point above sea level and this served as the living quarters for the visiting doctor and his assistants. The hospital, closer to the sea, was made out of three walls of tarred canvas with a roof of corrugated iron.

The sick and the dying had been provided with canvas shelters with open fronts and partially covered roofs, which could if necessary be turned with their backs to an oncoming wind. Dorré was similar in its layout, although there was no building allocated for a doctor.

I loved those islands; they were so fragile and innocent in spite of the use they were put to. They were not at all suited to human habitation and goodness knows who had chosen them as hospitals. They were nothing more than long strips of dead coral, like the vertebrae of giant snakes dumped in the Indian Ocean, with mud, sand and stones banked up on either side, no fresh water anywhere and only whatever plants and bushes could withstand the sun, the wind and the salt. All kinds of creatures lived there that had never seen human beings before. Banded wallabies and little marsupial mice would emerge in the cool of the evening. During the day the song of the curlew could be heard and sometimes I saw a wedge-tailed eagle. There were also snakes and lizards, including a legless variety that moved like an eel through the sand and a vast quantity of insects: clouds of them in the air, armies of them on the ground: mosquitoes, biting flies, stinging ants that would eat your shoes and clothes and even your toenails if you let them and ticks that would wait in patient expectant crowds along the line of drying seaweed. Those ticks were revolting. I once had a whole string of them black and shining around my waist, like a belt. I tried to get them off by scorching them with a stick taken from the fire but when that didn't work I had to wait until they were well-fed and ready to drop of their own accord.

By the light of the moon I watched turtles crawling ashore to lay their eggs in the sand, and little crabs that lived in mud holes would sometimes emerge like a vast rippling army of shells and claws. I remember once sitting and staring out to sea when suddenly there was an eruption of movement all around me and crabs were pushing their shells against my legs, my buttocks, the palms of my hands. It was so intimate it seemed to come from inside my own body, like a foetus kicking in the womb.

So there I was on those little islands, only for eight months but the time seemed so much longer than that. I had already quarrelled with the Professor before we got there and then we went on quarrelling. He would sidle up to me with his notebook and ask me all sorts of questions about what I had learnt over the years and once I had replied and he had written my reply down in his notebook he would gaze at me with a dazed, baffled expression, as if wondering what a silly woman like me was doing in the company of such an illustrious man as himself. He allowed me to act as his interpreter as if that was a favour to me and when I offered an opinion he would give me a tight smile and say something like, 'Why are all you women so muddle-headed, I wonder? Upbringing? Cranial size? A colleague once told me that a woman's brain is like a basket of wool in which a kitten has been playing.'

Radcliffe-Brown and his young assistant, Grant Watson, went to the islands first and I followed a few days later. When I arrived I found that he had already established a structure to work by. He had given numbers to all the patients – there were never more than a few hundred of them, they died so fast – and a canvas awning had been erected not far from the sea where he could conduct his interviews. I stood next to him day after day, angry but obedient, as one by one the sick were brought to us. Many of them were carried in on a stretcher, too weak even to lift a hand. Then he would ask questions which I translated for him and I would listen to their answers and tell him what they said. Kinship was an obsession with him and he used to get very cross if things were not quite clear. 'His mother's sister's husband? Are you sure, Mrs Bates? Are you quite sure?' If he was pleased with the way the interview was going he sometimes recorded the speaker on his phonograph and if he was especially pleased he would announce proudly, 'Now I am going to entertain you.' He would produce a record from his own collection and with great solemnity he would place it on the turntable and set it spinning. He was especially fond of Wagner operas; *Tannhäuser* was his favourite and I can see him now with his eyes closed and a smile on his face while the canvas awning flapped like a breathing animal and the air was filled with the buzzing of flies and the stench of disease.

It was extraordinary how oblivious Radcliffe-Brown was of his surroundings. I have seen him stepping over the body of a dead woman lying on the ground without pausing to notice that it was a woman who was dead. His assistant Grant Watson was different, he was very gentle and training to be a naturalist; I wonder if he is still alive. Sometimes he came to listen to the interviews, help with stretchers and so on, but he was upset by all those thin dark figures. He spent hours fiddling about with little pots and traps catching insects and he became especially skilled at catching ant-lions. I used to sit and talk to him sometimes in the evenings; he said he enjoyed the softness of my voice and like a child he would tell me everything he had done that day; the beautiful shells he had collected, the little wallaby that had bounced right over him while he lay on the sand, the contentment he found from sitting on his own and staring at the sea. Once on Dorré he came across two young black women, stark naked and red with blood, feasting on the flesh of a turtle they had caught but not quite killed. He said it waved its flippers at him as if asking for help and that had upset him more than the sight of all the diseased people in the hospital. I told him it was the nakedness of the women that had upset him, not the poor turtle.

It was while I was on the islands that the people started to call me Kabbarli, the grandmother. At night when I couldn't sleep, I would go and join them in their little shelters and they would ask me all sorts of questions about why they had been brought to this terrible place and what was going to happen to them and why was my son Radcliffe-Brown so afraid of them? I tried to comfort them but I also found that the sound of the sea was threatening and it was wrong to be on an island where people died but did not live. Sometimes at night I felt that the air was thick with the ghosts of all those who had been buried in the sand and who were now trying to return to their own country across the sea.

There was a terrible storm while I was on Bernier. The wind roared around us as it gathered more and more energy, the people in the huts were crying and even Radcliffe-Brown looked startled and uneasy. I took shelter in the hospital and the building stood firm although sheets of corrugated iron were torn from the roof and they clattered off into the night.

In the morning I went to inspect the damage. All those little sleeping shelters along the edge of the sand had been pulled to pieces. Some of the men who were too weak to move had been scattered along the edge of the shore like driftwood. I can see myself now, walking across that pale sand after the storm, looking at all those faces and not knowing what to do.

· *Thirteen* ·

I have been thinking about Eucla; calming my mind with thoughts of Eucla; a place where I was able to find a kind of quiet that was new to me. I still have a shell that I found on the white sands by the sea there. It was half buried in the sand, a little twisted island of mother-of-pearl, and when I bent to pick it up I disturbed a cluster of flies that were busy with the corpse of one of those strange spiny-backed puffer fish. A lot of them used to get washed up along the shore, scattered like pale inedible fruit rotting in the sunshine until all that remained were their bony parrot beaks and the porcupine spikes with which they defended themselves against their enemies – not that I could imagine anything wanting to eat a puffer fish.

So, the buzzing of the flies, the sharp but not unpleasant stink of dead fish and my beautiful shell which was surprisingly heavy, thick-lipped in order to survive the battering of the Atlantic Ocean. I kept it because it reminded me of the coastline: the sky, the sea, the white petrified waves of the sand-dunes and everything shimmering from inside as if there was a layer of mother-of-pearl just beneath the surface. All you needed to do was to scratch at it with your nails and there it would be, the secret revealed.

It was like eternity, that place. Something about the transparency of the light and the way the land seemed to merge with the air and the water as if the elements were interchangeable and the one could become the other. But it was also the silence. The muffled tread of a camel could be heard approaching from several miles' distance; thud, thud, thud, like a slow heartbeat. Sometimes for days on end the silence was so intense, so deep, that if it had been suddenly broken by the sound of something sharp like gunshot or a waggon rumbling across the hard ground then the shock of the intrusion would have made the land panic, made the earth split open to swallow us all into its belly. Curiously enough the sound of the waves beating along the shoreline never touched this silence, instead they seemed to intensify it, set out boundaries within which the silence was contained and magnified.

The people called the sound of the sea *Win-lya*. There were many songs that they would sing about it; that the old ones who could still remember the songs would sing; that they taught me to sing with them; that I sang to them sometimes, when they had forgotten the words. It is hard to translate these songs, in their own language they are so euphonious, so perfect and correct. There was one that I particularly liked singing, about the flood waters rushing across the land to meet the waves and how the two, the salt and the sweet, rolled over and over in each other's arms. I can't remember any more where it came from but I think it must have belonged to one of the tribes along the south coast. It went something like this:

Ancestor, ancestor
Me now they are kissing,
Again they are kissing, now they are kissing,
Again they are kissing . . .
Ancestor, ancestor, what do you want?
Swimming again, falling over and over
On the top of the foam, the froth and white feathers
Swimming again, roll over and over.

The wind could be terrible at Eucla. It blew in straight from the ice fields of Antarctica with nothing blocking its way or diminishing its strength. You could see the waves being sucked into shape one or even two miles out and then they would come rolling in, growing bigger and bigger as they approached, huge things battering themselves against the limestone cliffs, pushing up and over the high dunes. Then great chunks of rock would be broken off and you could hear them crashing down, at night especially, and I would wake up in the darkness thinking that the world had exploded. The freshly broken rock reminded me of old bones; maybe some of it was old bones, the skeletons of vast creatures that used to walk across the land long ago.

The wind from the sea would rush through the hollows in the rock, rush along the endless tunnels and passageways within the Nullarbor until it found a way through which it could escape into the open air with a great sigh, an exhalation. No wonder the people said that a snake lived under the ground, an angry breathing snake. They would avoid the blow-holes that can be found many miles inland all over the Plain for fear that the snake might grab at their legs as they passed by. They were quite right too: the Plain was terribly dangerous, a treacherous place, you couldn't walk there at night and even during the day a deep blow-hole could be hidden by a salt bush and suddenly there it was sighing to itself, a great mouth ready to snap at you. I only went exploring with guides and I respected their fear, shared it you might say. When the East–West Railway was built and the first of the trains rattled and screamed across the land with smoke belching from the funnel, the people said the snake had given up his underground home and had decided to do his hunting in the open.

I spent the first few months of 1912 quite close to the old telegraph station at Eucla. I have been told that you can still find the remains of my camp, although goodness knows why the sand has not covered it over. Even when I was there Eucla was almost a ghost town; a dozen or so white people, most of them old, clinging on because they did not want to leave but knowing that it was a losing battle. Until the turn of the century it had been quite a prosperous place with its own school, an assembly room, a wooden jetty stepping out through the shallow water, even a hospital and thirty telegraphers who sat at their desks all day sending out messages all round Australia: blip, blip, blipblipblip, wheat coming, sheep sick, war ended, gold found, ship wrecked, blip, blip, blipblip. But then the telegraph system was modernised, Eucla became redundant and the sand moved in to take its own. Now the graveyard has almost gone with just the tips of a few grey stones sticking out of the flood of sand and even the telegraph station itself is half submerged.

When I was there we had a bad drought, not as bad as some that I have known since but enough to kill all the livestock except for the camels which can live on anything. Even the rabbits died, lying in heaps as if they had all given up at exactly the same moment. It was a pity that so many of the kangaroos had been killed because they would have kept going in spite of the drought and then there would have been meat for us from time to time, but there were hardly any kangaroos left on the Plain, even then.

I stayed for a few months at a camp quite near Eucla. I was watched over you might say by an Englishman called Chichester Beadon, an old man who had a job as caretaker for the station which meant that he had nothing to do and was always glad to talk. He fussed over me and brought me food when he had it and the post when it arrived on the boat once every three months. He didn't seem to disapprove of me although he did worry about my safety.

Then I went further away, several miles along the coast and far from any whites. I left it to the Aborigines to decide where my tent should be pitched and when I needed to move on. I rather liked the uncertainty; not knowing what sort of view I would be given next. Usually we moved camp because someone had died. We had to burn the trees close to where the dead body lay and burn all the little shelters and then we had to move on, being careful not to walk across the tracks of the dead, careful not to gaze back at the place we were leaving.

For several months I was among the dunes looking directly out across the ocean, looking at Antarctica I suppose, if my eyes had been keen enough. Every morning before sunrise they would come and light my fire for me, waking me with the smell of woodsmoke and the soft pattering of their voices. Kabbarli is here. Kabbarli is with us. Kabbarli will feed us, protect us. With Kabbarli we do not need to be afraid.

I would make myself some tea before it was light and then sit out to watch the approach of the dawn, the bright colours heaving up out of the sea, the air still cool, no flies yet, the shadows sharp on the ground. Sometimes I found that I was crying, not because I was sad but because it was so beautiful.

There were about twenty Aborigines in the area when

I first arrived. One old man was the last survivor of the original Eucla tribe whose ancestral home was now occupied by the telegraph station, but there were others from the coastal tribes of the south. More turned up when they heard I had come to live with them, but it was always hard to tell exactly how many there were. Their shelters blended so well with the sand dunes and often you saw them only when you were about to barge into them. It was even hard to be sure of recognising a naked human figure moving through the landscape, they travelled like the shadows of clouds. I suppose that is why the authorities never believed me when I told them how many natives there were still to be found along the coast, starving and needing help. I had two hundred at one time and then they would go as quickly and quietly as they had come. But they left their old people and their sick with me and because of that I knew they would always come back eventually.

It was Koolbarri, the last man from the dingo totem, who took me to see the Koonalda Cave further along the coast. There is a huge underground lake there, I would guess it is as much as two hundred feet down and in the Old Time a man once lowered himself into the dark water using a rope made out of his own hair. The Koonalda Cave is a very sacred place. People came here to collect flints; they had been coming since the first beginning and even though everything is now very silent and empty there is still that sense of intense activity, as if they are all still there cutting at the walls of rock. Close to the mouth of the cave I examined some finger markings made with red ochre and thin geometric patterns cut into the rock which must have been done with flints I would think. They were such delicate twitchings of human life, like something a prisoner might have made, scratching with his nails on the wall of his cell to count out the days of his confinement.

· *Fourteen* ·

In Ireland I once saw a man lying dead on a table in the front room of his own house. He was wrapped in a white sheet like a new-born baby and I knew he really was dead because his face was no longer familiar to me, he was not the person I had known. They put salt on his tongue so that his body would not rot, they said, and to keep the Devil away; to stop the Devil from walking light-footed into his mouth to steal his soul. I remember how I stared into all the corners of the room looking for a creature small enough to stand on a man's tongue, perhaps jumping up and down in a fit of anger because the salt had spoilt his plans. Then the old women dressed in black who were also in the room started to keen, as was still the custom in Ireland when I was young; their voices as wild and strange as my own thoughts. I had forgotten everything about that day until one night at Eucla when I was woken by the sound of the women wailing for the man who had recently died at our camp and for as long as I heard their voices in the darkness I was back in my own childhood, staring at that white-wrapped figure and wondering what was going to happen next.

It is odd how one carries pockets of memory that you don't know are there until they are suddenly broken open, flooding the mind with a time that has ceased to exist. Eucla broke open so many of those capsules for me and each time it happened I was jolted back into something I had forgotten with such a sudden shock it was like falling down stairs. Then I had to sit quiet, rest my head on my knees and wait until a sense of the present reality crept up around me. The women were very kind, especially the older ones; they never said anything but they would pat me on the arm, stroke my hair, let me know that they could see me, that I was being watched over. It happened when the old man died at the dance and again when a woman I hardly knew was rubbing her baby with wood ash and I thought she was going to eat him just as I had thought they were going to eat that baby I had once seen in Ireland who was such a listless pale little thing but they all said he had the Devil in him, they could see it in his eyes. So they put him on a shovel, one of those long shovels they used for pushing bread deep into the oven, and they held him over an open fire to burn the evil out. He remained quiet and limp and when I screamed they turned on me and said maybe I had the same bad seed. Perhaps they were right, perhaps when I am dead my skin will go black just as the skins of the Aborigines will take on a shining whiteness.

We had so much singing and dancing at Eucla, more than I have ever known since. The music and the chanting of voices and the scent of green branches smoking over the flames and I would close my eyes and stand in a church with the priest's voice answered by the voice of the congregation; the priest holding up a wafer of flesh, a silver cup filled with blood; the people shuffling forward to eat and drink.

I loved to sing all those songs. It would be nice to make a book of them, an anthology, with the original texts on one page and the translations on the other so that you could have a sense of the rhythm of the words.

Warri wan-gan-ye
Koogunarri wanji-wanji,
Arri wan-gan-ye.

My country, my country, where is it, where is it?
This country I know not, its name I know not.
Wandering and standing I look far and far
Wandering and standing my eyes seek for it.
Wandering standing or dancing, wandering standing
My country, my country, where is it, where is it?

Towards the end of 1913 we all moved to Jeegala Creek which is about twenty-three miles east of Eucla. We went there because there was going to be an important dance and an initiation ceremony, a meeting of all the tribes from the southern coastal region. Many of the tribes had died out by then of course, but still about one hundred and sixty people were gathered together and we had members of the wild cherry totem, the wild currants, the nala tree which has a sweet-tasting edible bark, the sea-eagles who could scream like sea-eagles, the kangaroos, the emus, the mallee hens and others whose names I have forgotten.

The dances went on for fourteen days, dancing through the night and into the dawn and on and on. I attended every one of them, even the dances that the women were forbidden to watch, and whenever I could I made notes in my notebook, not very detailed but just enough to remind me of what had happened. We had chosen a clearing not far from the sea with a thick curtain of trees behind us like a backdrop in the theatre and numerous little fires were kept burning even during the day. It did look like a vast stage and at night it seemed as if this was the entire world; a platform floating in space with figures dancing upon it, their naked bodies flickering in the firelight.

It was very licentious, very sexual; the men dancing naked in front of the women, the women dancing naked in front of the men. I remember a group of young women moving in a long line around the outer circle, hardly seeming to lift their feet from the ground; their thighs quivering like fishes, their knees knocking together. I sat and watched with the older women, beating the ground with green branches and singing the songs which told how the first people had come to this continent.

Sometimes the dancing was performed in little groups. I was by one of the fires with Kitty, Jira, Dhoondoo and Mary and five men came to dance before us, white-painted stripes glistening down the length of their thighs, across their backs and chests. Even the old men could dance with an extraordinary beauty, shaking and swaying like the branches of a tree in a storm. They paraded in front of us with that high trotting step, their backs straight, their arms clenched to their sides and then they turned to face us, pointing their wands at us. There was one old man, a member of the nala totem who died while he was dancing. I thought he had fallen into a trance and he was left unattended for several hours. In the light of the dawn I saw that he was cold and silent and when I went back to my tent there were drops of water falling from the nala tree which grew close by, even though the air was clear and there were no clouds. I called to a friend to come and see what was happening and he said that the tree was weeping for the dead man and since it was my tree it was an indication that I should be made a member of the nala totem group.

You must understand that although I was with the women, I was not a woman. They told me that in the Old Time I had been a man, a tribal elder, and now I was neither man nor woman, I was a supernatural being who had moved beyond the boundary of the sexes. There was a sacred enclosure that belonged only to the men and if a woman approached it then all the men had the right to possess her. Even if she died as they swarmed over her body it was forbidden to protect her or avenge her death; but I went close and was not harmed. Often the women had to go away before a dance was ended, but I was allowed to stay and witness the secrets of the men.

When the fourteen days of dancing had come to an end I was able to take part in a men's initiation ceremony and I was made into the Keeper of the Totems. I was woken before the dawn by the sound of boomerangs clicking and I stepped outside my tent to be confronted by fifty men standing in a half-circle before me, waiting for me. They each carried a spear and they were naked but decorated with a head-dress made out of cockatoo feathers, their bodies painted white and red, hair belts around their waists, the tassels red with blood.

The camp was silent because the women and children had moved far away. I took up my position in the centre of the group and in single file we followed a track that went along the edge of the cliff. Fires had been lit on either side of the track with men standing by them and beating the flames with green branches so that we walked through billows of thick smoke. Two of the men who were with us broke the silence with the sharp cry of the eagle-hawk but apart from that we were quiet. We reached a cleared space where a huge fire was burning. I was given a mallee branch to hold in my right hand and I sat with the others in a semi-circle on the ground. We beat our branches on the ground and when one man shouted *Yudu* everyone except for me closed their eyes. I saw a tall man with a long black beard approach the fire, holding a totem board that was more than twice his height. The board was deeply grooved and painted with geometric patterns and the figure of a kangaroo. The man lifted it up above his head as a priest might lift up the host before the altar and then he lowered it carefully to the ground and stretched his body across it. He rose and carried it towards me and touched the wood against my breast, my back, my shoulders and my knees and then laid it down before my feet. This ceremony was repeated twenty or thirty times as the leaders of the different totem groups stepped forward and set their boards down before me.

When it was over I walked in the centre of the group and we carried the boards to a storehouse. They had previously been kept in a cave but this cave had been discovered by some white men who had stolen a number of sacred objects and now the boards were given a temporary hiding place. I helped to lower them one by one on a bed of fresh mallee leaves and when the work was done we carefully covered the entrance of the storehouse so that no one would suspect what was hidden there. I was now the Keeper of the Totems and it was my duty to grease the boards and freshen them and make sure that no white man came to disturb them.

Some people have refused to believe that all this really happened. They have said that no woman could ever have been initiated into the ceremonies of the men, that no woman could have seen the sacred dances that I have seen. I have tried to explain that, although I am a woman now, I was a man in the Old Time and the people treated me as if I was a supernatural being. But if I am not believed there is little I can do to prove that what I say is true. All the friends who were with me at Eucla are dead now, I don't know of a single one who is still alive today.

· Fifteen ·

It must have been while I was at Eucla that I killed my husband; killed him in my mind I mean and told people who asked me about him that he was dead, poor man. I even felt a certain tenderness for him which was something I had not known before and on the table in my tent I put up a framed photograph of him as a young man, next to one of my son when he was a baby.

I gave birth in the upstairs room of a hotel in the town of Bathurst with no clear understanding of what was happening to me and only the wife of the hotel manager to help me. While I was in labour, clinging to the cold metal rungs of a rickety bed, Jack was outside in the yard wrestling with a Welshman for a bet of £20. I kept very quiet in spite of the pain and I could hear the two of them grunting and roaring down below and the shouts of the men who had gathered to watch and must have put money on the fight. It was Jack who won and he rushed into the room all sweat and loud talk just as the baby was bursting out of me. I would gladly have murdered him if only I'd had the strength. Told him so as well but I doubt if he heard.

Anyway, at my campsite a few miles east of Eucla I wept real tears because my husband was gone for ever and once I had removed him so thoroughly from my life I found that he appeared quite often in my thoughts. I would look at the photograph and remember him as he had been when we first met; how thin and strong and how he had stared at me. At night as I lay in my tent I would sometimes imagine that he was lying there beside me although I could never clearly picture his face. The sound of the wind rushing in from the sea and buffeting against the limestone cliffs was the sound of his breathing and the darkness of the night air pressed down on me like his naked body. I had three dreams about him all in the same week but after that he disappeared from my sleeping life. In the first dream he was the skeleton trapped in the tree, laughing. In the next dream he and I sat down at a table to eat our own child who was brought to us on a white dish like a roasted chicken. And then I had a dream in which he approached me with extraordinary gentleness and said, 'Everything you have done and seen I have done and seen with you; you have not been alone.' It was a strange comfort to me, making it seem as if there had been some point of contact between us after all.

Not that I have felt alone during all these years. I have learnt how to be very close to the people I live with and there is no aspect of their lives that I have not shared; the secrets of the men and the secrets of the women. I have seen them dancing, dying, making love, giving birth and I have never once been excluded from what was happening, never once made to feel like an outsider gazing into a forbidden territory. Sometimes when I look at them I seem to be seeing myself and when I am told a story or confronted by a particular landscape it is as if I knew about it all along but had briefly forgotten.

I had been in Eucla for about two years when in March 1914 I received an invitation to go to Adelaide to attend the British Conference for the Advancement of Science. A number of important people were going to be there, including my old enemy Radcliffe-Brown, and I had been invited because of a paper I had written about the West Coast aborigines. I saw it as a turning point; the value of my researches would now be recognised and the government authorities would be bound to make that recognition official by appointing me as the Protector of the Aborigines for South Australia. I would then have a steady income, respect from strangers and a chance to help my natives in the best possible way. It was not to be of course, but I was not to know that, not yet. The future might follow a fixed course but luckily we can never see where it is leading us.

In those days a steamship made a regular journey from Fowler's Bay to the port of Adelaide but there was no easy way to cover the 240 miles along the coast to Eucla. I arranged to hire a buggy and two camels from the local storekeeper at Eucla. He was very kind, he said I should stay for a few days, I would benefit from some white talk; he would sleep in the front room of his little house while I could sleep in the same bed as his wife. I felt something like panic at this offer and realised that I could never again sleep in the same room as anyone and certainly could not share a bed with a housewife. Also I knew I had to be careful how I made the transition between the black and the white world. It has to be done in stages, like a diver in one of those metal capsules who is slowly pulled up out of the depths of the sea, pausing as he adjusts to the different weight of the air around him.

I left my tent standing in the camp with all my possessions

in boxes and trunks. I packed a blue silk dress – a beautiful dress that was so well-made – a white linen suit, the hat with the pansies, shirts and gloves, best boots and best silk underwear, study papers, a handbag and a toothbrush that I had kept in its protective wrapper for several years. Everyone at the camp, even the sick and the old, thought themselves an ideal companion for the journey but I chose a woman called Gauera and her fourteenth husband, a man called Balgundra. Her thirteenth husband, Ngallilea, who had sold her only recently, met us along the way and decided to come with us; this worked well even though it was not according to plan. The people lit a big bonfire on the morning of our departure so that the smoke could follow us as we disappeared into the distance. Some of the old ones wept because I was going and they had grown accustomed to having me with them, looking after them during the day. 'Kabbarli must talk with the elders of her tribe,' I told them. 'She will return with food and gifts, you must wait for her.'

Big fat Gauera had been along the coast several times with previous husbands but for the two men and myself it was all new, although we had learnt many of the songs and stories that belonged to the places we would see. We were to follow the tracks that cross the edge of the Nullarbor Plain from water hole to water hole, keeping quite close to the high cliffs, crossing what I am told is the oldest existing land surface in the world, and you could feel it too, everything there was cut through and through with memories, every rock, every bush saturated so that there seemed to be no room for the present time, only a crowded past jostling for attention. Even the tiny plants that would shrivel and die after a few weeks seemed infinitely old, I suppose because they were growing on the ground that belonged to their ancestors.

At Head of Bight the cliffs come to an end and you must enter an undulating ribbon of white sand-dunes that shimmer and seem to change shape like banks of cloud in a clear sky. The camels could imagine that they were back home in the deserts of Arabia, the hot sand comfortable under their padded feet. Then we would cross a wooded marshy country that went as far as the salt lakes of Yalata and on to Fowler's Bay. The journey could be completed in two weeks if there were no rain storms and no accidents, but I allowed myself almost two months because I did not want to miss the conference.

Sometimes all four of us sat on top of the mountain of luggage, lurching this way and that with the stride of the camels and the bumping of the wheels on the hard ground. We stared out across the hundreds of miles of the Plain, a blur of soft colour. The land looks very much like the bed of an ocean, it's so flat and still and you seem to float above it and stare down, even if you are walking. There are no trees, only clumps of low shrubs and bushes. I made a list of all the ones I could name and it reads like a poem, or perhaps an incantation: saltbush, bluebush, samphire, billy button, spear grass, silver grass, blue grass, cotton bush and shells, shells everywhere. There are ripples of movement on the bare patches of sand which must be caused by the wind, and the taller bushes have their branches pulled away from the direction of the sea as if they were being tugged by an underwater current. You can find lovely fossils, perfect white scallops embedded in pieces of limestone, looking as if they have just been swept ashore by the last tide, and those funny cylinder shapes that I think are the bodies of some kind of squid. One day Gauera took us to see what looked like a muddy pool but it was a smooth sheet of stone with footprints walking across it: a large creature with splayed toes like a great lizard and a line of six human steps where a man and a woman walked in the soft mud when there was not yet such a thing as the Nullarbor Plain or the high cliffs breaking off at the sea.

There was no wind for the first few days and as we travelled we sang songs which told how the ancestors came here and the songs which told how the land had been made. The porcupine whose body turned into the sharp porcupine grasses that can slice into the flesh like a knife; the twin boys whose father hurled them out to sea where they stand as an island of two steep rocks with cormorants and sea eagles nesting on their shoulders and in the crevices of their bodies. We passed the earthworks of wombats; huge and systematic excavations as if a group of archaeologists were busy with the first stages of uncovering a lost city. I kept a wombat jaw bone, mottled with patches of bright yellow lichen and looking like the twisted branch of a dead tree. Balgundra caught one and said, 'Look, it is like a human baby, if you press its hind foot on the sand it leaves the mark of a human baby crawling.' Even in death the wombat has a comfortable and contented expression; dreaming of underground palaces and the white roots of trees that it can bite through with strong jaws. We roasted it on the fire and it tasted delicious, like pork. We also ate a little brown bird called a tawny frogmouth that looked like a bundle of twigs when you placed it next to a bundle of twigs, I believe it is almost extinct these days. And the tail of a sad-eyed wallaby that had sat to stare at us as we went past as if it had never seen a human being before and certainly never guessed at the danger it might be in. And a huge carpet snake that Balgundra carried into the camp draped over his naked shoulders like a grand lady with her fur stole. Gauera told us that when she was a child her mother killed all of her other babies because there was no food for them and so she was fed on her own brothers and sisters; at least I think that is what she said.

Gauera was full of stories. Sometimes we would walk beside the camels to stretch our legs, but she said she was much too fat to walk and so she would sit above us like a queen, laughing, telling stories and shouting insults at the camels. She smelt of pleasure, a ripe musky scent that I am sure was the reason why men found her so desirable. I told her that a man could follow her trail like a dog fox following a vixen, but she found nothing extraordinary in the idea. She was one of the few of her people who did not see me as a creature who had no sex and she used to tease me, saying it was wrong for me to have no one to kiss. She gave me a piece of mica that a man uses when he wants to capture a woman. He makes it reflect the glare of the sun into her eyes so that it strikes her like lightning and then she runs this way and that trying to escape. She moans and cries and is lost in the bush and far from her own tribe and after two days she must follow the glint of the mica that will lead her to the man.

I was sometimes very sad at night; a great sadness would blow over me like the wind coming in from the sea and the sound of the wind seemed to be the sound of myself crying and desolate. Gauera and her husband used to sleep close to my tent while the man Ngallilea went some distance from the three of us. Big Gauera with her breasts and belly gleaming in the moonlight and then it could seem to me as if there was no canvas separating us and I was lying with her husband, laughing in the dark. I did see them together sometimes but they didn't mind; he kneeling in front of her and she on her back with her thin legs clasped around his loins.

Several people have tried to find out about such sexual matters from me because they knew that I must know a great deal. There was a man called R. H. Mathews who wrote to me in 1905. He began with compliments about my dedication and how brave and fearless I was for a woman and was I never afraid especially at night? He said he would live with the people just as I did, but unfortunately it was not possible because he had work to do and would I mind clarifying a few questions for him. He began by asking about legends and customs and I told him everything I knew, because I was glad to be asked and it never occurred to me that he might steal my work and call it his own. Then in September 1905 I received a letter from Mr Mathews with neat pen and ink drawings of penises all down the margin, I've still got the letter and I can quote from it. 'Dear Mrs Bates, please excuse the indecent and obscene drawings, but we must get the facts. Could you tell me, Mrs Bates, from your experience, do the women drink the semen of the men? And have you perhaps heard the women say that they get more pleasure from the sexual act when the penis has been mutilated as in Figure 2 with the line of incision marked ABCD or when it has been mutilated as in Figure 3 which during erection creates a curve along the line marked ABC? These things may seem very horrible to us, Mrs Bates, but you must appear to think of them as excellent customs and in that way you will be able to "hammer out" all the information we require. I would do it myself if only I had the opportunity. Dear Mrs Bates, I hope your health is good and that you are eating enough of the right food, no one can live on bread and jam.'

I never answered the letter and I wrote back a few weeks later as if I had never received it. I thought of Mr Mathews when I was travelling with Gauera. She could have answered all his questions and others that he had not even dreamt of, if she had agreed to talk to him. But why should she? It was none of his business, he could never understand the private dealings between men and women in the way that I could.

It took us five days to cross the Nullarbor. We lit fires along the way and sent smoke signals to any wandering people who might be in the region but there were hardly any. We passed native graves at Koorabi and elsewhere and the graves of six white people at Nundera with a little rock plant of vivid Irish green growing close by. It made me think of an oasis in the desert; I would be glad to be buried close to such greenness. When we reached the sandhills the camels travelled easily and seemed to lose their usual gloom but I was soon exhausted. It was like crossing a great glimmering ocean with the waves of sand seeming to be about to swallow us up, to obliterate all traces of our passing. The fiery north wind blew a layer of sand into our faces and cut more fiercely at uncovered skin than the porcupine grass. One day I amused myself when we stopped to rest by seeing how long it took for an object to be buried by the sand. A tin cup disappeared in less than a minute, a blanket in five, but then I was too tired. I was so tired I couldn't even sleep at night. Once I was lying in a daze in my tent and I became convinced that I could hear the monks from the monastery at Beagle Bay, singing the chant for the Office of the Dead in their thin soft voices, and I wondered if they were singing it for me. I even saw them, walking single-file across the desert, coming to fetch me, and I felt a strange elation, a contentment that I hope I will know again when I am really dying.

Then we were through the sand and into the wooded area. This was orphaned country; the people who belonged to the region had died out or had been driven away by farmers and settlers. We met a few straggling groups who were making their way east or west, but they were not travelling in the old sense, they were listless and confused like refugees caught in a war, escaping from one danger but knowing that they were heading towards another.

After twelve days we reached Yalata, and my three companions set off back the way they had come. I had been given the name of a farming family called Murray and I stayed with them in their house for five weeks; my acclimatisation I called it. I had my own room and a bucket of water so I did not need to share the family bathroom. I used a billy can to boil water over an open fire in the morning when I was making my tea but sometimes I joined the family for an evening meal. They were not intrusive if I was silent or if I went out walking along the coast for several hours, especially in the evening. Slowly I felt my civilised skin growing back and then I was ready to take the boat to Adelaide.

I wore my blue dress when I arrived and I had already cabled a couple of newspapers, including my friend Hurst, the editor of the *Australasian*, so there were several journalists waiting to meet me and eager to interview the lady who lived with the blacks, the lady who had crossed the Bight in a camel buggy. They took some nice photographs and everyone who interviewed me told me that I was nothing like the person they had expected; I was so elegant, so aristocratic, I appeared like an apparition of wealth and sophistication, it was impossible to imagine someone like me living in a tent in the bush, travelling with only blacks as my companions. They all noticed how young I looked and I laughed and said that all my grey hairs were well covered by the little hat with the pansies on it.

Three days after the Conference had started, war was declared in Europe. The Conference was not cancelled but people were suddenly too preoccupied to bother themselves with the thought of what was happening to the Aborigines in the south and who might be the best person to act as their

Protector. In July 1914 I gave evidence to the Department of the Interior and I explained how the Aborigines were suffering and how the women in particular would benefit if I was appointed to help them. Some members of the Department said that they doubted if there were any Aborigines at all in the area along the coast and certainly not as many as I had estimated. The decision to appoint a Protector was postponed indefinitely.

I went with the Conference to Sydney and Melbourne and then in September 1914 I made my way back to Yalata. I chose a guide to accompany me and I set out with two camels and a buggy towards my camp at Eucla.

· *Sixteen* ·

I wish I had a photograph of Fanny Balbuk. I miss her and would so much like to see her again. I used to think of her as my grandmother; she reminded me of what I can remember of my grandmother, the same stubborn chin, the same tone of voice, the same way of staring into your eyes not so that you felt trapped or threatened but just that you knew you could be seen, all the complexities of your soul could be seen and still it didn't matter. When she was telling me stories she would hold on to my sleeve or the hem of my skirt and tug at it if she sensed I was not concentrating. She died in 1905 and since I had no photograph of her I thought I would like to keep her skull, but I never got it. I suppose it would have been awkward to pack and easily broken and anyway the skull of a good friend would not provide much comfort when one was feeling lonely. Sometimes here in the desert when a baby dies the mother places the body on a termite hill so that the ants will eat the flesh and then months later she can return to collect the fragile bones. I once saw a young woman weeping as she laid out the tiny skeleton of her baby just as you might do a jigsaw puzzle, assembling the picture piece by piece.

Fanny Balbuk had grey-dark skin and very white hair, cut short with a stiff fringe. She had the habit of frowning and pursing her lips forward when she was on her own, as if she was wrestling with a private despair, but she always smiled easily in company. She had small, dry, paper-soft hands and I made everyone in the camp laugh so much when I examined the lines of her palm and said I could count all of her husbands there; the ones she had already grown tired of and the ones who were waiting for her in the future. Pointed toenails, hard and black as ebony and as sharp as the claws of a hunting dog. I have seen her draw a pattern in the sand with the nail of her big toe: an almost naked old lady balanced on one foot, drawing a beautiful geometric pattern with her toenail, an intricate cage, a labyrinth fit for a minotaur. I wish I could draw like that.

In a way she was all the things that I am or that I would like to be, only much more clearly so, she never felt the need for concealment. She was a bigamist, just like me, but she went seven times to the altar of a church in New Norcia with a fresh husband on her arm and no one noticed or asked her if she was the same person now as she had been then. Maybe the priest couldn't tell the difference between one black face and another, just as Jack said he couldn't although I never believed him. I wonder if anybody would have noticed if I had married Jack in the same church in which I married The Breaker. I hardly dare to think of him, poor man. He was so wild and beautiful, smelling of honey, and when I learnt that he had been shot by a firing squad with his back against a wall I had to hide my sadness very carefully.

Fanny Balbuk came from the Perth region. She was

the last of the Black Swan totem, or was she a Kangaroo, I am not sure now. It was her grandmother who was buried under the huge weight of the government buildings in the city centre and she would rattle at the gates and scream to be let in, shouting curses at passers-by. She told me how she had gathered edible lily roots in the deep swamp that is now the Perth Railway Station and whenever I arrive at that station I seem to see her wading naked through the mud among crowds of white strangers, her shouts like the cries of marsh birds.

She had her own shelter on the Maamba Reserve, wouldn't sleep in a government hut and built herself a little lean-to out of a sheet of corrugated iron and a few pieces of wood so that at night she could feel the wind and see the stars and the moon. I used to visit her regularly and write down all the stories she told me in her soft voice. She must have been quite old but she seemed to be strong until one day her totem animal walked close to where she was lying and then she knew that she would die soon. At the end they took her to the hospital in Perth, although I told them there was no need, I could stay with her and help her. But no, they put her in a bed and shut out the sky. She was only there for a short time and one morning she shouted until she had summoned a doctor to her bedside. He was a young man and not unsympathetic and she looked him in the eye and said with a terrible authority, 'Ninety-nine!' Maybe it was her way of accusing him of having brought her to that cold house. I doubt if she was afraid, even at the end; she knew all about death and how she was going to make a journey under the sea to meet her family on the other side. I used to think of her walking on bare feet among the fishes, the rocks and the waving plants until she arrived at the place where she was going and could pull off her black skin, just as I pull off the tight warm silk of my nightdress. I hope she was able to leave this world, it would be awful if she found she couldn't escape from Perth and had to go on hammering at the gates of the government offices.

Her husband came to the camp with the news of her death. He looked like a ghost himself, walking so slow and smooth. He stood before his wife's nearest relative, not saying a word and sat upon his lap, facing him with one knee on each side. He held his right hand under the man's thigh, he pressed his naked chest against the man's naked chest, the side of his face to the side of the man's face. The women watched and I watched with them and we all knew at once that Fanny Balbuk was dead. They let out a cry, a lamentation of women such as must have been heard all over the world for thousands of years. The keening of women that has always haunted me.

I have here before me a copy of a letter that Fanny Balbuk wrote to her son, a half-caste called Joe Donelly. I had forgotten that she had any children and I had forgotten that her one child was a half-caste. She always said that she hated the smell of half-castes more than she hated the smell of white men; or was it me who said that, I am no longer sure. Anyway, when she was growing old she began to miss her son, just as I miss my son, and she longed for him to come and live with her, to watch over her more carefully than a husband ever could. This is the letter she wrote: 'Dear Joe. When will you come down to see me. I hope you will come while I am alive . . . All our people are dead. Jimmy Shaw and Billy Shaw your two uncles are the last that have died. George Totwon is dead. You remember him? He was a jocky. Bob is dead too. He used to work for Carmichael. Jinga is dead. Tchamtcham is dead too. Now I think I've given you all the news.'

I copied the letter into one of my notebooks although I can't think why unless perhaps I helped her to write it.

Immediately under it I have written, 'I sing. You sing. He is singing. We sing. They go. You and I go.' I am glad that I kept so many notebooks, they make it possible for me to return to all the details of the life I have lived, enter closed doors and walk along corridors and through rooms that have been left standing empty. Just a few words or a few lines on a page and at once the floodgate is opened and it all comes back to me. There is more to remember of Fanny Balbuk from that note or from her stories than there ever would be from her skull. Still, I would have liked a photograph; then I could invite her to sit with me in my tent, keep me company the way she used to, make me laugh, come and spend an evening with Sir Francis and Lady Newdegate and Lord and Lady Forster.

I was sorry to have not been with her when she died but I am sure she did it well and with great dignity, death is not always sad. After my trip to Adelaide and all that business with the British Society for the Advancement of Science, I spent a lot of time with people who were dying and it was a very happy time, for them and for me.

My first camp when I got back was in the hills west of Fowler's Bay, quite close to the sea. I was there with the remnants of many groups from the eastern, western and northern edges of the Nullarbor Plain. It was absurd of those government officials in Adelaide to suggest that there were no people along the coast in need of help, there were dozens of them, hungry and sick, but no one wanted to be bothered with the responsibility, they were too busy with the war in Europe, it made me very much alone in my task.

I had two old men and one old woman who were blind and as helpless as babies and because they had been deserted by their next of kin they depended on me to look after all their needs. I decided that the four of us should go and live somewhere on our own and so I led them a few miles inland to a place called Wirilya. I had a long pole which they could hold on to and in that way I led them. Some friends came with me carrying my tent and provisions and they built a breakwind for me before they left.

Wirilya was a little haven, a paradise in a way. My tent stood in a grove of acacia trees and I could look out towards the coast across a soft sea of mallee bushes. There was a good deal of rain, not like now when the rain seems to have given up; the rock holes were filled with clear water and all sorts of flowers burst out of the sand and out of dry twigs and branches. The mallee bushes seemed to be endlessly covered with a haze of yellow fluffy flowers and little yellow caterpillars pretending to be flowers. In my memory I can hardly distinguish between the quivering heat of summer and the floating mists of winter, they seemed to tumble after each other like night following day. In my diary I made a note of how 'the sunsets blaze and fade and blaze again' and watching them was like listening to a wonderful music that pulled at me and almost made me long for death.

I was there at Wirilya with my three old people and a young woman who came to find me and somehow two or even three years passed by. I saw no one else except a few little groups who never stayed long. The land was criss-crossed with paths made by animals, birds and reptiles. We had wallabies and stiff-legged turkeys, a few wombats, lots of snakes and lizards, and shy marsupials you could watch scuttering about in the early evening. Then there were the white animals as I called them, the new arrivals like foxes and rabbits and the wild cats that were more fierce than anything else this fragile country had ever known. Every-where you looked you could see the evidence of a past time when the sea had covered the land. Near to the coast I found some more fossilised footprints; birds, animals and humans walking across what had once been soft mud, hunting for each other I suppose, or for the oysters and big mussels that were now hard stones embedded in the limestone.

I was busy every day between dawn and sunset, scrabbling like a terrier dog in the sand, digging out rabbits and lizards for our food, cutting wood, lighting fires, cooking, caring for my people. I had to light their pipes, rub their aching limbs, and reassure them in their darkness. Sometimes I would take them for a walk, holding on to the pole and following me like a line of ducklings.

Dowie was one of my blind men. He was completely demented and he would have fits of extreme madness when the moon was full. He could not tell me anything about his life but I gathered a lot, perhaps people told me or I just knew. He was like a son to me, a mad, bad son. He had been a cannibal of the wildest sort. I know for a fact that his mother gave him four of his baby sisters to eat and she rubbed his body with their fat; that was when he got his taste for human food. He grew to be terribly strong and fierce and he threw sand in his mother's eyes so that she was blinded and he beat her with sticks and stones and hated her and all women and most men. He killed and devoured the flesh of at least eight wives and he ate anyone who tried to stop him; he would go hunting for human flesh just as a man might hunt a kangaroo. Then his sins caught up with him, as you might say. He lost the sight of an eye and one night when he was out in a wild storm his brain snapped, just like it did for King Lear; he ran screaming through the wind, no one daring to approach or help him. Later he lost the sight in his other eye and although he was still fierce people ceased to be afraid of him because he could no longer catch them.

He often wandered at night. I used to be woken by the sound of his screams and find him entangled in the ropes of my tent like a trapped animal. Or he would wander off into the milky light of the full moon and I would have to go in search of him. Once I hunted for him for five hours and walking through that pale blackness was like walking in a dream, the bushes seemed to move and breathe and the land shone with a phosphorescence such as you sometimes get on the waves of the sea. I found him cowering and naked, but he wouldn't come with me so I had to bundle him onto my back, supporting myself with my digging stick as I stumbled towards the tent. I am only five foot four and he was a tall man, but somehow I did it. It reminded me of a dream I had when I was a child, in which I was carrying an old man who clung to my shoulders and I was making my way towards the moon but I kept falling, with him falling with me and never releasing his grip.

Dowie died shortly after this and I dug his grave with a scoop and digging stick, working through the heat of the day until I had made a hole seven feet long and five feet deep. It was I, all alone, who lowered the body down and a grey shrike thrush came to sing at the grave: a fitting farewell since the shrike is a cannibal bird that eats fledglings whenever it gets the chance.

After I had been at Wirilya for a year or maybe more a young woman arrived. She had walked two hundred miles to find me, although a kind dingo-trapper had given her a lift for the last stretch of her journey. She was in her early forties, the same age I had been when I first came to the desert, but she looked much older, even older than I was by then. She was dying of venereal disease given to her by a white man or by many white men, she must have been very beautiful once.

I gave her brandy to drink, I rubbed her body with

oil and lanolin and I kept her warm, lying in the soft sand with a fire burning on either side of her. She was not like Fanny Balbuk, she had no idea of where she might go when she was dead, no confident expectation of walking under the weight of the sea, arriving safely in a land on the other side. I told her that my father would look after her but I never knew if I meant my father who had gone to America or my father who was supposed to inhabit every Christian church. I also told her she might meet a good friend of mine called The Breaker, she would recognise him at once because he smelt of honey and he would be kind to her. The next morning I carried her body into the shade of the acacia trees and I dug her grave and buried her.

It was all too much for me, of course it was. I started to have terrible headaches that seemed to pierce my skull, I could feel them thrashing about like snakes inside the hollow cavity. I couldn't sleep any more at night and there came a time when I could no longer tell the difference between my dreams and my waking hours. I think that once a man who could not walk crawled on all fours into my camp, smiling, with the body of a carpet snake wrapped around his neck and shoulders. I think I was visited by three naked women who had live dingo puppies tied around their waists with hair string and they were smiling too. When the moon was full I thought I would go as mad as Dowie, crashing through the night, terrified by the sound of my own stumbling feet, my own cries. Then, like Dowie, I would cower somewhere by a bush, waiting to be found and brought home, but there was no one to find me because my companions were blind.

Before things got any worse I arranged for a letter to be carried to my friends the Murrays at Yalata. They were good friends and within a few days a camel buggy arrived to carry me back to their house.

· *Seventeen* ·

I have been sorting through the metal deed boxes in which I keep my papers. I cannot find Mr Radcliffe-Brown's letters but I will have another search when I feel better. I am still so tired although the worst seems to be over; if only we had some rain then I am sure I would recover at once like a tree that looks as if it is dead but can burst into life with the first taste of water.

I must remember to write to Mrs Hill re desert; the man-made desert that is spreading across this land like a disease. I have decided to make a plan of the years from 1899 onwards; I am sure it will be useful to Mrs Hill or to anyone else who wants to know where I have been and what I have done. Sometimes I am afraid that I might lose the thread of my own movements, but things always look clearer as soon as they are written down. My work in the Eucla district ended when the Great War ended in 1918; it was then that my strength gave out and I had what the doctors called a severe breakdown. For a few weeks I was in a hospital in Adelaide with all the wounded soldiers and then I stayed with friends. People were very kind.

My work here in Ooldea began in 1919. It must have been the month of September when I arrived: spring flowers in the red sand and on the thin branches of the trees and I knew at once that I had come to the right place. I have been clinging on ever since; a limpet that grips even tighter to its rock if you try to dislodge it; a very determined lady who will not let go, regardless of what her enemies say or how they try to threaten her.

It is true that I have suffered terrible hardship during the last sixteen years but there have been many rewards as well. Yesterday three half-caste children came to my camp: two boys and a little girl who was so pretty, so bright, so bubbling with natural intelligence. I would like to adopt her as my daughter and then I could teach her how to continue with my work but it would be too complicated, especially now. I gave them bread with the last scrapings of my jam supply and they seemed pleased.

Chocolate. I must get some chocolate from the store and collect my Western Mail receipt. Send cheque to bank. I have only four oranges left out of six and no apples last week but half a dozen lemons. 'The writer has lived in Ooldea for almost seventeen years and it is the only life she is fit for. She has adopted these people so that it seems to her that they are her family, her poor relations. She may be the last person to ever witness their dances, their old ancestral dances. She has seen the passing of the last members of so many tribes and groups. She has tried to comfort them and she has helped to bury them, lowering their frail bodies into a hollow in the sand. Even here close to her tent there are many graves. The oldest and most interesting race of people in all the world is passing away before her eyes and sometimes she wonders if she is passing away with them. Perhaps she will go ahead of the last comers and wait for them to arrive on the other side, a familiar figure waiting to welcome them.'

I am planning to leave Ooldea in a few days. I have packed most of my things and there is not much more that needs to be done. Then I will stand on the concrete station platform and watch for the approach of the train: steaming and roaring as it cuts across the Plain connecting the east to the west, the west to the east. I will be travelling on the same train that brought me here all those many years ago. The guard or some kind gentleman will smile when he sees me standing there, so small and ladylike; he will offer to lift me up onto the high carriage steps, his strong hands holding me around the waist. I will be wearing my best grey suit which I have just finished mending, my little hat with the pansies; people will know at once who I am. In this barren land I will appear to them like an apparition, an oasis in the desert and they will make comments about my elegance, the quality of my clothes, the sweetness of my voice. There will be those who are keen to talk to me, 'Would you mind, Mrs Bates, if I sat here next to you? I have heard so much about you and there is so much more I would like to know. Champagne? Please, allow me – this meeting is a cause for celebration.' I will let myself be caught up in all the questions and in that way I will not need to think too much and will hardly notice the landscape slipping away beyond the carriage window.

Whenever I leave a place I am reminded of the moment of arrival; the intensity of those first impressions resurfaces and merges with the intensity of departure so that the intervening time is swamped and seems to have hardly existed. When I go from here I will leave something of myself behind; a ghost waiting for the return of its body. Even if I manage to avoid looking out of the window I will know that I am reflected in the eyes of the people who have come to wave goodbye. My people. When you see them walking naked out of the desert they appear like kings and queens, princes and princesses, but standing barefoot on the edge of the railway track, dressed in stiff and stinking clothes, black hands held out to receive charity from white hands, then they are nothing more than derelicts, rubbish that will soon be pushed to one side and removed. My poor people, how will they manage once Kabbarli has gone? Lost without Kabbarli.

When I took the train from Adelaide to Port Augusta and then on from Port Augusta to Ooldea I felt as if I was coming home. Bookaloo, Woocalla, Pimba, Wirramina, Kingoonya; all the stations along the line have been given Aboriginal names although the land around the stations was already orphan country even then; no one left to remember its history or to sing the songs of how the world began. You could see it straight away, a sadness on the land like the sadness in the face of a child who has no parents.

Construction work on the track had begun in 1912 and it was completed by 1917 but there were still a lot of men for several years after that. At the height of construction there were over three thousand men employed. They had to lay two million five hundred thousand sleepers, they had to shift five million cubic yards of rock and earth with pick and shovel, camel and carthorse in all that heat. Some of them went mad; a time-keeper disappeared for five days and when they found him he was walking in circles round and round not far from the camp. They brought him back but he was soon off again and the desert swallowed him up. Sometimes they had to sleep out in the open like Aborigines, or they would curl up in concrete pipes, little huddles of them like a pack of dingoes. They drank whisky mixed with methylated spirits, they gambled and fought and fornicated with the black women who were so easy to obtain all along the line, so quick to learn the secrets of civilisation. The flies were terrible; the buzzing blackness of flies feeding and multiplying among the hectic human activity. And crows, they said that great flocks of crows would arrive out of nowhere and descend on the new rubbish dumps.

I like to imagine what it would have been like to look down from a great height to watch the line being built. Men like ants scurrying this way and that, a rippling mass of activity pressing forwards, the metal train tracks shining in the sun like the mark a snail leaves when it crosses a stone. An earthworks gang went on ahead; they needed to be as much as a hundred miles in advance of the track layers when the land was difficult. It was their job to clear the way; push earth and sand and shattered limestone to one side and remove the scrub and trees that stood in their path, stacking up wood for camp kitchens or for the locomotive fireboxes. It's odd to realise how many good-sized trees used to grow here. Apparently there was once a forest of black oaks around the Ooldea Soak and now you rarely see a single one. During a dry season people used to collect water from their spidery roots; those trees stand so lightly on the ground, you could almost push them over with your bare hands. The myalls have mostly gone as well, they have a dark dense grain and they burn very slowly leaving the finest of white ash. The smell of myall wood always makes me think of raspberry jam; the finger-plates on the doors of the first-class carriages are made of it; it shines like the best mahogany when it is polished.

It was relatively easy to fix the train tracks into the smooth limestone of the Nullarbor Plain, but the area around Ooldea caused a lot of technical problems because of the sandhills; the beautiful red sandhills that reach back into the Great Victoria Desert where they go on rolling into the distance for hundreds and hundreds of miles. The sand is fine and powdery, not like the pale crystals along the coast, and it can move forward with the strength of floodwater. The men had to push these red waves back to one side and it was as if the desert was putting all of its energy into blocking their path. They would make some progress during the day and then at night a wind would come and blow all their efforts to oblivion. One storm raged for twelve hours and even at midday the sky was so thick with red dust that it was as dark as night. But they got through in the end; they constructed ramps of galvanised iron that deflected the power of the wind, they faced some of the cuttings with slabs of stone, they kept on and on, just like ants.

Mr Bolam the station manager told me that they found several blind sand burrowers when they were digging through the sandhills. They are such strange-looking creatures, with soft pink noses and silky yellow hair like a baby's, and they live as much as twelve feet under the ground as if not yet ready to be born. Mr Bolam kept one in a cage. It would race around the limits of its prison at a desperate speed and then suddenly fall down and sleep, as if a switch had been pulled that disconnected it from the waking world. It did the same while eating: collapsing into the food dish, fast asleep with its mouth full. When it died I put it in spirits and posted it to the Natural History Museum in London. They never sent me a letter of acknowledgement which I thought was most odd, I had such a nice letter when they received the five barking lizards. I am sure that the people here must have failed to send the package; they have been very cruel to me, especially recently. I know for a fact that my post has been tampered with and I suspect that some of it has been destroyed. I wonder if they read it before destroying it?

When I arrived at Ooldea in 1919 there were still perhaps a hundred men working for the line. A passenger train and a goods train stopped once every day and about twenty whites were living close to the Siding: fettlers and their wives, the postman, the storekeeper, the station manager. I was surprised to see how much rubbish had been left lying about and no one thinking to clear it up as if the desert was some kind of vast abandoned building site. There were heaps of broken machinery, smashed concrete pipes, empty crates and boxes, stoves and cooking pans and pieces of furniture. I remember finding three white dinner plates and a pair of shoes placed very tidily next to a bush, far from any sign of human habitation. Quite near to the Soak I came across what looked like a shrine set up to appease a difficult god: a wooden stepladder with a bucket on the top step and two spoons, a train ticket and a broken statue of the Virgin Mary carefully placed inside the bucket.

The Soak is about three miles inland from the Line. There is a ring of high sandhills surrounding a patch of paler sand but nothing in particular distinguishes the place or makes it seem remarkable. There used to be many more trees of course and I was told that clumps of green rushes grew around one of the old waterholes, the bitter soak that was used for healing the sick and curing all sorts of skin ailments. The whole area must once have been crowded with life, but that is all in the past now, even the rabbits have died out recently: the place is filled with memories that stretch back and back in time but have been snapped off in the present, like a twig.

The railway land surveyors knew that there was water to be found somewhere beneath the sand but they had no idea how much or whether it was good to drink. The first bore that was sunk in 1916 brought up a bitter liquid that was not even fit for the camels, but over the next few years they established a total of fifty wells, with nineteen of them providing pure sweet water. By the time I arrived they had installed a pipeline that carried a supply to the track and then along the track, east and west for several hundreds of miles, enough for many thirsty people and many thirsty steam trains. At the height of production ten thousand gallons of water were being sucked up and pumped away every day. That lasted until 1926 when the supply ran out and the Soak was officially declared empty. There must have been a huge underground cavern lined with a bed of clay to make it impermeable and I suppose the fools bored a hole right through the clay, letting the water drain back into the cracks and holes in the limestone, like a bathtub running out. Or it could be they simply took too much. Either way the fact remains that the Soak is almost dry and can only provide a couple of shallow pools of water that fill up slowly if you dig into the sand and then seep back to where they have come from.

I like to imagine the hollow area that lies beneath the sands of Ooldea. I see it as an underground palace, the ceiling held up by thin pillars of rock, the walls smooth and waxy, the floor marbled with the coloured clay that you can sometimes find here: white and yellow, brown and violet. I turn on a light and I can walk through the echoing chambers, run my hands across the silky walls. I turn on a light and my palace is filled to the brim with clear water and I am swimming in this cold and silent lake, my white skin glittering like the scales on the body of a fish.

I had my camp quite close to the Line for the first few weeks after I had arrived, but once I had got my bearings and had made arrangements with the white people about collecting food and mail, I moved a mile or so inland to a small sandy gully on the track that led to the Soak. I was right next to the pipeline and for as long as there was water I had a tap from which I could collect my daily needs; it seems like an extraordinary luxury when I think of it now. I built an enclosing breakwind of mulga bushes and I set up the little household that has been my domain for all these years.

Just as I had expected, the remnants of numerous tribal groups had converged on the area, perhaps as many as several hundred, while a slow drift of men, women and children were still walking in from the northern deserts. There had been a severe drought in Central Australia during 1914 and 1915 and that was forcing the people to move southwards in search of food and water, but it could take them several years to come this far. There were others who had made their way to Ooldea because they had heard rumours about how the great snake of the Nullarbor was no longer in hiding, he could be seen, racing across the land. They said that the dead with their white skins had come back to the land of the living, there was new food to be eaten that did not need to be hunted or searched for and a new drink that made the head spin.

I was there looking back into the desert and forward at the Line, like Janus standing guard at the gate of heaven. I lit fires to send signals to the new arrivals so that they came to me first and I could prepare them in some way for the changes they would have to confront. I gave them food and clothes and I tried to warn them about the danger, especially the danger to their young women, but I could never persuade them to return to the places they had come from. They were all hypnotised by the metal snake.

· *Eighteen* ·

I look around at my tent, round and round at my tent. Trestle table, stiff-backed chair, trunks and boxes, cups and saucers, best clothes hanging in white bags, second-best clothes in a trunk under the bed. My worldly goods stare down at me as I lie here; friends who have come to visit the invalid, come to pay their last respects perhaps. I cannot speak to them because it is too hot; I can only smile and nod my head in acknowledgement of their presence and their concern.

Outside the sky is blue and flat, flat and blue and as dry as a bone. I gaze at a narrow triangle of sky where a corner flap of the door has been tied back. I wonder if that is an isosceles triangle or is it the one whose name I always forget in which the right angle is equal to the sum of the angles of the other two sides? Long ago I was told that if only I could get a grip on mathematics then I would have a grip on the real world. An odd logic, but I suppose it made sense.

All that heat and dryness beating down outside has

soaked into the canvas; my tent is a dried husk and I am the seed rattling inside the husk, waiting for rain. When it's as bad as this even breathing is painful; hot air creeping down my throat as if it would suffocate me. It's amazing that my tent can survive such a battering from the sun during the day and then attacks from the frost at night. Here at Ooldea I have seen how slabs of rock can be splintered and turned into sand by the alternations of heat and cold. Maybe I'll wake up one morning to find that my tent has cracked open and then I'll have no protection from the bright eye of the sun. But not yet. I have mended the places where the canvas was torn after the last wind storm and yesterday evening I checked the kerosene cans to make sure they were all well weighted and firmly in position, holding my house down around its edges.

There was a drought during the first year that I was here. Nothing like as terrible as the Long Drought but it was all new to me then and it enabled me to learn about the limits of my own endurance; what it is possible to do and what it is not possible to do in certain circumstances. You could call it my initiation ceremony, my ordeal by fire, and when I had come through I was one step further towards something, towards being black I suppose. If those Germans down at the new Mission Station were to know just how black I have become they would be very busy with me; washing my mouth out with soap; beating me just as they beat poor Alice for stealing a ripe pomegranate that had fallen to the ground; threatening me with a hell-fire much worse than anything the sun can achieve.

Alice is at the Mission school now. She is being taught all about sin and its many disguises and she told me she has learnt Thou-Shalt-Not-History and Thou-Shalt-Not-Geography. In a little while she will have her grip on the real world and then she will be ready to walk up and down the East–West Line exchanging the use of her body for a bottle of beer or some tobacco if she is lucky. I told someone recently that the Mission school is a training ground for prostitutes and beggars, but they didn't want to understand me. I tried to explain how confusing Christianity can be, like showing a hungry child a room full of cakes and then slamming the door shut, leaving the child in the cold dark. I have often been in the cold dark myself, so I know what it's like.

The Lutheran Mission has been built right on top of the Ooldea Soak, stamping the new onto the face of the old in the same way as the early Christians used to build their churches on the sites of pagan temples. They have got dormitories, a chapel, a school and a big storage shed for all the government food rations, but although they say that this is the beginning of a permanent settlement here I doubt it. I would like to come as a spy fifty or even sixty years from now, to see what has survived and what has disappeared. A few broken water pipes perhaps, sheets of corrugated iron, lumps of concrete, but not much more. Maybe the pomegranate tree will still be struggling to keep going in the red sand but I am sure there will be no white people living here. I wonder if I would have difficulty in finding the place where my tent stood? No, surely not, I could always find it, even after a thousand years. I would say, 'Look, these rings of rusted metal in the sand are all that is left of the kerosene cans which held my tent down, and here is a mother-of-pearl button that I lost a few days before I left, and here I had my kitchen and here were the steps to the observatory from which I would watch the stars.' If any of my people are still alive in the future then they will be sure to know this place too; maybe it will have become sacred, the Dreamtime Campsite.

The Ooldea Mission is run by a woman called Miss

Annie Lock. She arrived in 1932 with her friend Miss Reid and nothing has been quite the same since. She looks exactly like my childhood idea of a Hun: a flat, unbaked and almost featureless face, a huge heavy body and arms strong enough to swing the big axes they use to fell the trees. Her cheeks turn bright red when she is angry and she spends a great deal of time being angry as if she thought that was a way of getting things done. Although I am sure she washes regularly she always smells of sweat, a sharp oniony smell. She insists that the people wash as well, scrubs the children as if she was trying to whiten their skins although I have told her that it hurts them so much.

There were no missionaries in the region when I arrived but I crossed swords with a number of people who were determined to put a stop to my work; Germans mostly, this part of Australia is riddled with Germans, in spite of the War. Mr South was my worst enemy. Some fool in Government appointed him as the official Protector of the Aborigines, although, as I told him, the only thing he was interested in protecting was his own pocket and his reputation as a dedicated bureaucrat. He hated the Aborigines, 'They infest the East–West Line,' he said, as if they were vermin, and I became vermin as well because of my association with them. It was Mr South who tried but failed to have me driven out of Ooldea in 1920 and it was thanks to his efforts that I was refused any further government help and was branded as an eccentric, a liar, 'the woman who lives with the blacks'.

Then there was Mr Bolam the Station Manager, the one who kept a sand mole in a cage. He seemed quite kind in his way and I felt sorry for him because of his stutter, listening patiently while he hobbled through his sentences. I encouraged him to write a book about the region and let him use my notes about the people, the birds and the wild life that belong here, although he never thanked me once the book was published. I had presumed that he would support me when there was all the trouble, but he was on the side of the enemy, just like the rest of them. 'Mrs Bates and myself work along entirely different lines. Whereas I like to assist the natives to be independent, Mrs Bates likes to entirely kill their initiative and make them entirely dependent on the government.' That's what he said, I saw a copy of the letter and after that I never spoke to him again. I often walked right past him as if he was invisible.

I had only been settled at my new camp by the water pipe for a few months when there was the Railway Strike. That started on 3 October 1919 and lasted for fifteen weeks. All the white people along the Line between Kalgoorli and Port Augusta were told that they must leave as soon as possible because when the trains stopped running there would be no more food supplies and no way of getting out if you needed to. They tried to persuade me to go with them but I said I couldn't; I had eight sick people who would die if I did not care for them and someone had to stay to make sure all the others who wandered up and down the Line would be provided with food if they were hungry. I sent a wire to Adelaide asking for government stocks to be sent to me to deal with the emergency and when nothing came I arranged to obtain some supplies from the store at Cook, a station a few miles on and I bought whatever the fettlers and their wives had to spare, because they couldn't take everything with them. I had a good quantity of flour, tea and sugar and a barrel of porridge, so I knew I would be able to manage for a couple of months, or even longer if necessary.

In an odd way I rather enjoyed the Strike. I called it my War Effort and I became so thin and dry that I felt as if I could be carried by the wind like a dead leaf. Apart from the two pumpers who stayed on at the Soak for the first few weeks, I was the only white person to be found for hundreds of miles east and west and then the pumpers gave up the struggle and set off hand in hand to walk to Fowler's Bay and I was on my own.

I hadn't realised until then how threatened I felt by the presence of white men. Because the Line made a connection between the east and the west, packs of them would move across the country like scavenging dogs and then there were the outcasts of the pack, the solitary ones who were even more dangerous. I kept my revolver under my pillow at night and carried it in a pocket of my skirt during the day. Sometimes when it was dark and quiet I would imagine that I could hear a man creeping hungrily around my tent; then the canvas of my tent became like a thin curtain that I only needed to pull back to reveal I don't know what horror on the other side. I had seen so many women and young girls who had been raped and beaten and so many bodies ravaged by the effects of syphilis.

But with the Line silent, no trains passing and no men wandering, I had a new freedom. I slept naked in my bed at night and when I got up in the morning I would not hurry to get dressed and cover my nakedness. I wore my best silk underwear every day during the Strike and that was a luxury that compensated for the shortage of food.

There were still so many birds around then, and lizards. I would be woken by the watery burbling song of the desert thrush, 'woorolooloo, warawaralooloo, woorolooloo'. Little finches had made their nests in the breakwind so that the dry branches seemed to shake and twitter with life. I had a dingo dog that had been caught in a trap and a cat called Lady Kitty who became so wild and promiscuous that I had to get rid of her. I had six horned devils, little spiky lizards that were wonderfully skilled at catching ants;

each one had a piece of red thread tied around its neck, so that the people knew they were mine and were not to be stolen. I also had a bicycle lizard who looked as fierce as he was gentle; he became so tame that he would creep up onto my lap and sit there, basking and catching flies. There was a chameleon as well but he was never so courageous and would watch me from a corner with his swivelling volcano eyes.

I lived mostly on porridge, making a big pot of it three times a day and sharing it with anyone who was hungry. I had expected a crowd to come to Ooldea for a corroboree in November but they never turned up. Still I had a lot to deal with, between twenty and forty men, women and children to care for at Kabbarli Camp. When they could they brought me offerings of food; an iguana one day, a mallee hen's egg the next. Water was a problem because I had to carry it back from the Soak and that was a long walk in the heat with temperatures well over a hundred degrees. I didn't mind, although I can remember the pleasure of eating fresh bread and butter when the first train came through in December.

When the white people returned to Ooldea they treated me very badly. They had always been suspicious of me but now because I had stayed on without them and had survived it was as if they had proof that there was something wrong with me. I was not natural, I was like an old woman who is accused of being a witch because she did not die when they tried to drown her; like that child I saw long ago who was put on a hot shovel because they wanted to burn the devil out of him. I kept my dignity and my distance but people laughed openly when I had to walk near them and they shouted terrible obscene things. Sometimes the train would stop a little way past the station so that a crowd of passengers could wave and jeer from the carriage windows.

In March 1920 Mr South came to visit me with a police-man and a young fettler's wife who sometimes brought my mail and had never been unkind. Mr South said that if it wasn't for me there would be no black people at Ooldea; I enticed them to my camp with offerings of food and I tried to force them to stay because I wanted to be surrounded by a swarm of black men, black naked men who I wanted to have close to me and he laughed. He said that I buried the bodies of the dead in the sand near my tent so that their ghosts would frighten away my enemies. He told me that although I was a Justice of the Peace I had no authority anywhere and I would never be made an official Protector no matter how I begged or threatened the people I thought were my friends in high places, because everyone knew I was nothing but a crazy old woman. He had already appointed a pumper from the Soak to hand out food rations to the natives if they came begging, so I had no function any more and he demanded that I leave the area. I kept myself very calm and ladylike and I told him and the constable to leave my camp this instant, now, immediately, or I would shoot them, and I produced my revolver. Afterwards I was so shaken that I went blind for three whole weeks; a black mist around my eyes and I had to move on all fours, groping for familiar objects. Mr South, the constable and some other men had chased all my people away. Not inland where they might have been safe, but down the Line where everything was so dangerous for them. The woman called Nyurdigulas gave birth to her baby prematurely because of the fright and for eight days it lay with its eyes closed and not long after it died. She became a prostitute along the Line, just like all the others, and when she gave birth to a half-caste she killed him and ate him. I blame Mr South for that, cannibalism is his fault and the fault of men like him. No one wants a prostitute with a mewling child clinging to her neck, or they give birth to babies that are the wrong colour, or they kill them to protect them from harm, just like rabbits do, so I am told.

In those early days I still thought I could do something, I thought that if only I could establish a camp away to the north, far from the Line, then I could keep the people out of danger, I could warn them and prepare them and maybe they might even decide to stay away from the white men. I wanted to go to Windunya Waters, one hundred and forty miles inland, but I could never do it on my own and it was impossible to persuade anyone to believe in my plan and help me. Towards the end of 1920 I remember how I watched as a family group of twenty-six men, women and children approached my camp. They had travelled down from the Musgrave Ranges, over a thousand miles inland, and there they were, naked, smiling, glistening in the sunshine. I tried so hard to keep them with me, but I couldn't do it. They all drifted down to the Line and then they were gone.

· Nineteen ·

I couldn't sleep last night. I lay on my back and stared at the stars until I seemed to be out there with them in the darkness. The sky was breathing; I could feel the cavity of the night expanding and contracting around me as if I was in the belly of the universe. It has been so quiet recently with no one to talk to; even the birds and lizards have deserted me, all except for the butcher bird but I wish he would go away and leave me alone. In the afternoons I sit and watch the shadows of the trees and bushes lengthening across the red sand. Sometimes I get up out of my chair and move forward very gently so that my own shadow merges with them and for a little while I can feel as if I have turned into a bush or a tree. Each day ends abruptly with the setting of the sun and then we can all die together. Just at the moment when the sun goes down there is often a violet afterglow, a sudden flare of unnatural light that illuminates the sky for an instant. I have never seen it anywhere else, except here in the desert.

A family of mice has established itself in the box of

diaries I keep under my bed. I hear them rustling about and occasionally there is a fierce squeak; I rather like their musty, intimate smell. I pulled the box out from under the bed to look inside and inspect the damage. They have been eating the leather covers of some of my diaries and they have made themselves a beautiful nest out of the thin paper on which I kept a record of the days of my life. They must have torn the pages into strips with their teeth. I opened up their bed of words and there at its centre was a tangle of pink naked babies, but I didn't have the heart to throw them out. The butcher bird would be sure to get them straight away; he would nail them to a tree and devour them at his leisure, just as he has done with my finches. I am sure he would eat his own young if he had any, but even the butcher birds have given up mating and nest-building in recent months.

I have decided that I will spend this day remembering the occasion when His Royal Highness the Prince of Wales came to visit me here at Ooldea. No, not here, it was further along the line at Cook; they decided that would be a better place for him to stop, although I don't know why, it was most inconvenient. This was in July 1920 and the Prince was travelling on the Commonwealth train from Adelaide to Perth as part of his royal tour. Consolidating the Empire after the War, that is what he was doing and he did it very well, he was such a nice man. He had his own coach with a real bed in it instead of a bunk and I would have loved to step inside, take tea, talk to His Majesty, sit on the edge of his bed. But there was so little time, only a couple of hours and he was off and we were all waving as he disappeared into the distance.

In spite of all the recent trouble with Mr South I was asked if I could arrange an entertainment for the Prince. No one else could have done it so they had to ask me and

I was glad to see that at least my work was appreciated in some quarters. The tribes in the Ooldea region were very scattered because of Mr South's interference, but I managed to collect one hundred and fifty of my people together. I explained that the great King of England was coming to see Kabbarli and he also wanted to see the fine things that Kabbarli's people could do; how they could dance and sing, how they could weave string out of human hair, how they could cut flints, grind seeds. They were unwilling at first until they realised they must do it for my sake and I promised them a great feast once it was all over. 'My King has told me that he will feed you well,' I said.

I collected all the things we needed for the occasion: kangaroo fur, human hair, feathers, paint, stones, and other ceremonial equipment, boomerangs and other gifts. Then we set out to Cook in the train. We were provided with the cattle truck that was used for transporting goats, the floor permeated with the stink of goat, and we had to huddle together as closely as animals being taken to the slaughter. I felt as if I had become the manager of a travelling circus, but instead of lions, tigers and elephants I had tribal elders and newly initiated boys, old women as thin as sticks and young women as soft as peaches. I even had to bring my sick patients with me, three women including Jinwilla who was blind and that other one whose name I have forgotten, who died just after the Prince left.

We arrived a couple of days early to give us a chance to get everything ready. Cook is a terrible place; it has none of the diversity of Ooldea, none of the sense of the past crowding in around you. There is a flat plate of limestone that looks as if it was only recently covered by the ocean and there is nothing else: no trees, no bushes, no rolling sandhills, not even any colour; just hard, lifeless, broken ground under your feet and an expanse like a nightmare of infinity on all sides as far as the eye can see. There is a row of about eight little houses made out of tin and concrete, a school room, a shed that is called a hospital, a village store, and nothing for people to stare at except each other.

A little crowd was waiting on the platform when we arrived and they watched us with sullen faces as we clambered down: thin faces, creased and lined by the intensity of the sun which they say is even fiercer at Cook than it is at Ooldea. I kept myself aloof. I knew that I needed to maintain a certain distance and dignity because I had been chosen to entertain His Majesty. A fettler's wife summoned up the courage to ask if I would like to stay as a guest in her house, but I said no, I am quite all right thank you, you are very kind but I prefer my own accommodation. My people drifted off into the landscape and I busied myself with turning the goat truck into a bedroom. The floor was filthy but I cleaned it with some newspapers and had to use a sacred woman's totem board as a dustpan. I made myself a bed out of blankets, I hung up a piece of white calico cloth as a curtain and I built a little fireplace of stones outside in the dirt. I had my own bucket and I heated some water with which to wash. Then I felt much better.

I knew that newspaper photographers would be accompanying the Prince and there was also talk of a cinematograph which would relay the occasion to the cinemas of the world. I decided I would look my best in black: a black suit, a black hat, white gloves and a white shirt. On the morning of the day of the Royal Visit I washed and dressed with great care and when I was ready I felt as if I was a royal personage myself. It was a pity I had so little time with the Prince. With more time I could have told him about my childhood and how I once met his grandmother, quite by chance in a garden. I could have shown him my

Royal Umbrella that was picked up and handed to me by his uncle the Duke of Gloucester, long ago in 1900, when I was not such an old woman. 'But you do not look like an old woman to me,' the Prince would say. 'You have the energy of a young girl and you look so much younger than in the many photographs I have seen of you. But tell me, dear Mrs Bates, how can I show my gratitude for all the work you have done in preparing this entertainment?' Then I would smile and say to him, 'I have one request, Your Majesty. Let me visit your bedroom carriage on the train. I have often wanted to enter the bedroom of a King, or a future King like yourself.'

It was a pity that we were at Cook and not at Ooldea. At Ooldea we could have danced our sacred spirit dance at the Soak and the red sandhills would have towered above us like the tiered steps of an ancient amphitheatre, while the firm pale sand of the Soak would have been our stage. Instead we were out in that flat land and I was allocated an unmarked area not far from the Line. 'But the Prince must have a royal platform!' I said and although they tried to disagree they realised I was right. I supervised the construction of a dais made out of a pile of wooden railway sleepers. Once it was ready we had a rehearsal with a railway employee taking the part of the Prince, gazing down at us from his castle ramparts. I joined in with the dancing and the singing in order to share and communicate my enthusiasm. I have always loved the Yuala spirit dance, which was why I chose it.

The train stopped half a mile from the Siding at three-forty-five precisely and the Prince and his suite alighted. I can see him now coming towards me on a white horse. He is galloping and the hard earth trembles at his approach. He rides as if the horse's body was his own, just as The Breaker used to ride when I used to ride with him. But he stops before he reaches me and turns to inspect a group of soldiers who have lined up in front of him, silent and geometric. I don't know where these soldiers suddenly appeared from, I suppose they might have been travelling with him on the train. They stand very still and the shouts of their commanding officer echo across the Plain like gunshot. Then, at last, the Prince turns and comes closer, but his horse has gone. He climbs up onto his platform and he looks down at my cannibals who stand to attention, waiting for my word of command. It was Lord Claud Hamilton who presented me to His Royal Highness and when I had curtseyed His Royal Highness requested me to join him on the dais. I climbed up the big rough steps and there I was standing next to him while the photographers took their pictures. I gave a sign and my people gave a shout of welcome. Then the women began to sing, the men began to sing, the men and women began to dance, high-stepping and swaying to the music while I explained the symbolism of what was happening to the Prince who was fascinated.

When the performance was over we had a demonstration of our native skills and the Prince stepped down from his platform in order to see things more closely. He watched as old Janjira wove a length of string on her naked thigh and I don't think he would have realised that she was blind if I had not told him. He watched the grinding of seeds, and when Marburnong demonstrated the making of a flint axehead, he asked if he could try and Marburnong guided the royal hand. Two young initiates were brought forward, shy and proud, their heads heavy with their elaborate headdresses. The Prince was given gifts: a boomerang, some little carved figures. I had thought of giving him a pair of murderer's slippers but I changed my mind at the last minute because I was not sure what he might think of them.

The festivities ended with the booming cry of the bull-roarers. The Prince had been with us for almost two and a half hours. I wish I had kept the photographs of the two of us standing side by side. I only have the newspaper cuttings and they have become so faded and fragile, I hardly dare to touch them for fear they might crumble to pieces in my hands.

Then he was gone and the night fell as abruptly as it always does here. The whites went back to their houses and my people and I had a feast of roast sheep which we cooked over a big fire. It must have been on that same night that Joongura died, although I am now confused about what we did with her body. Did we bring it back to Ooldea on the train or did we somehow manage to bury it in the hard limestone, digging a hole in the darkness? I seem to remember that I did not sleep at all that night. I had bought a candle from the fettler's wife and by its dim light I read one of the works of Dickens until the dawn came. *Our Mutual Friend* it was. I could never do that now, my eyes are not strong enough.

Those early years seem crowded with visitors, although I suppose there were not so very many. I used to arrange to meet people who were passing through and I would talk to them for an hour or more before their train moved on. Then there was Miss Pink who came with her box of watercolours and stayed for three days and Miss Ruxton who was a friend of the Governor of Western Australia and she stayed for five days and wrote a long but not very clever account of her visit in the newspaper. I felt very lonely when she had gone.

Who else? A group of anthropologists turned up one day and seemed friendly enough but then after we had talked for a while they offered me twenty pounds, as if I was a beggar in need of their charity. Jack never came, of course not, he must have been dead by then, but my son Arnold was here, briefly, once. I was standing on the platform at Ooldea, waiting for I don't know who, and I stared up at the crowds of faces in the windows of the carriages, men and women, looking at me or looking away. And there was Arnold, next to a window in a first-class compartment, I saw him quite distinctly. Our eyes met and interlocked with such a passion, as if we had been lovers, but then the train began to move away and I lost him.

I sometimes think he came a second time but I am not so sure; it is not a happy memory. He was there at my campsite but I couldn't let him enter my tent because he was a man and no man can enter my tent. Then he had nowhere to go and there was nothing I could do to help him. I gave him some blankets to lie on under the open sky within the shelter of my breakwind and I hope he slept peacefully. I expect he will write to let me know when he wants to see his mother again.

· *Twenty* ·

They call the mountain-devil lizard ming-ari, which means full-of-ants. The females are much cleverer than the males; it is only the females who know how to scratch at an ant nest so as to bring out a fresh supply of angry soldiers. When I had my little flock of ming-ari to keep me company I saw that each individual could eat as many as a hundred ants in an hour. I have watched one of them standing on an ant 'road', eating and sleeping throughout the day until she was gorged and there were no more ants left to trickle past her. Sometimes the ants fight back, swarming over the body of the lizard and trying to find a patch of skin that is soft enough to bite into. The ming-ari are good stoics when they are under attack like that; they stiffen their matchstick legs, they puff out their bodies so that their spikes bristle in all directions and they stand very still, swaying slightly as they wait for the invasion to come to an end. They have only one vulnerable point and that is the lower lip; if they are bitten there then they toss their heads from side to side just like a fiery racehorse who resents being made to wear a bridle.

When you study something as intensely as I have studied my lizards, they can take on a huge size. I have seen them turning into dragons as big as palaces. I have seen their eyes flashing, their nostrils breathing fire, their skin encrusted with bright jewels, pulsating. And when they fight I have heard the metallic clash of their jaws meeting, their tails beating on the ground.

Long ago the ming-ari were a tribe of women who did not want to mate with men. They had wild dogs living with them for protection and if ever a man crept too close then one of these dogs would spring at him and tear him to pieces. The ming-ari were a travelling people who needed to move on as soon as they felt their hearts growing hot from sitting still. They would journey across the great deserts carrying their babies on their backs and whenever they rested they would leave some of their babies behind, warning them that they must not speak or whistle otherwise men would find them and try to mate with them. Some of these silent children turned into the stones beside the waters where their mothers had stopped to drink. These places are known as ming-ari waters.

Then it happened that the star man Nyiruna decided that he must have these stubborn women as his wives. He tried to entice them with offerings of food and when that failed he chased them over the earth and up into the sky where they were turned into the stars that we call the Pleiades, while he was Orion, the one the Greeks call the hunter who was killed by the goddess Diana although I forget why she did that. I still watch the stars at night from my wooden observatory and I can see how Orion the star man longs to get closer to the Pleiade women, but they always refuse him, taunting him from the safety of distance.

Mountain devils are able to live for several weeks without

any food. I suppose all desert creatures must have the ability to suspend life and wait for change, just as I have learnt to do. On days when it is too hot to move, each lizard makes itself a tunnel four or five inches long and it remains there until the intensity of the heat has broken. I once did a rather cruel experiment and exposed one of my lizards to the sun on a very hot day. Its skin turned a bright yellow colour with a few reddish-brown patches and within minutes the poor thing was dead. I sent it to the Natural History Museum, along with a note telling them what had happened because I thought they might be interested. When it was very cold my lizards would make themselves a deep burrow in which they might remain for a month or more, but on cool days they loved nothing better than to lie on the warmth of the palm of my hand. In some dialects the man's penis is called *birant*, little lizard, while the woman's vagina is *yemerr*, little black lizard, but those must have been a different species to any of the ones I kept as pets; smoother, more snake than dragon. It was when I was looking through my papers that I came across this information and on the same page I had made notes on the names given to the fingers of the hand. The thumb is the hand-mother, the first finger is the hand-father, and then comes the eldest brother, the middle brother and the youngest brother.

Bicycle lizards are gentle and easy to tame but they can seem very fierce during the mating season. The female potters about drab and indifferent as if nothing is happening while two males are busy fighting for her and might even die in the fight. The colours on their bodies blaze red, yellow, blue, orange and black. They stand erect on their hind legs and advance towards each other, their mouths stretched open like fish out of water. The aim is to slash and tear at the head of your opponent and although I never interfered when a battle was raging I did often nurse the loser back to health, feeding him with flies and spiders, bathing his wounded mouth with a mild antiseptic.

I have noticed that neither the bicycle lizard nor the mountain devil show any affection to their young. They simply hide the leathery eggs in the sand and leave the little ones to hatch and fend for themselves. The night lizard is quite different. Both parents watch over the babies, feeding them and protecting them from danger. But in a fight the night lizard will devour his rival's tail if he gets a chance; swallowing it down still twitching with what looks like immense satisfaction. Sharks eat each other of course, and rats. My cannibals do as well, particularly the women with their new-born infants, although I do my best to stop them. I sent a baby's skull to Professor Cleland at the Adelaide Museum to prove that I was right about cannibalism, but he said it was only the skull of a cat, which is absurd. Long ago I once dreamt that I had eaten my own son; I roasted him in an oven and felt very uneasy when I woke up in the morning and remembered it all.

I wonder what I would choose to be if I could be something other than human. Certainly not a lizard, but a bird maybe. The bell bird who used to sing to me at dawn or the white owl of the Nullarbor, a ghost with the face of a cat, gliding so silently through the dark sky. They say here that when someone dies their spirit sits in a tree and presently a bird's voice is heard. Then the relations of the deceased talk to the bird. 'What is it that has happened? Why did you die? Where are you going, my son?' And the bird who at that moment is the spirit of the dead person answers them. 'I am going away,' he says.

No one spoke to Jajjala when he died because he was a member of the dingo totem group and they do not speak to the spirit of their dead, not even during the first hours when it is still very close to the body. The dingo totem group have to make their way to a cold country somewhere in the west. It never seemed like a very attractive place to me and when I was told about it I was glad that I was not a member of that particular totem.

Jajjala died of syphilis here at Ooldea, white-feller sickness they call it and everyone was so sad because he was the youngest male relative in his family group. I think it was in July 1922 and he was twenty-five years old; such a nice young man and I had got to know him so well that I felt as if I was his own mother when he lay cold on the ground before me and I was helping to prepare him for burial. During the final days of his life one of his brothers always sat next to him, a hand resting on his heart so as to feel the delicate reverberation of his heartbeat. All the people were gathered around close to the breakwind where he lay, crying softly in anticipation of what was going to happen. When he died their grief became loud and desperate; although I have seen so many deaths and burials I don't think I have ever seen such passionate despair. The men hurled themselves on the ground and the women lay on top of them; a heap of naked bodies moving like an anthill. Some men stood up and clasped each other, body to body, shouting to the sky. Some of the women rose up and placed the sole of their foot on the head, the back, the shoulder of Jajjala's father or one of his brothers. Two women pressed their naked bellies together so that they could share each other's sorrow. As the evening drew in fires were lit to the east, the south and the west of the breakwind. There was no moon that night but the stars were everywhere, brighter than any moon.

The gravediggers each took a lighted firestick from one of the three fires and they ran around the place where the body lay, carrying their flaming torches and crying as they ran, 'Pah! Pah! Pah!' I had been sitting next to Jajjala but

I went with the gravediggers to the hill where he would be buried. Fires were lit along the way and the men shouted the sharp dingo cry, a yelping cry as if the dog was caught in a trap and was calling for help.

The grave was dug to a depth of nearly seven feet and it must have been five feet long and four feet wide. The sand that had been scooped out was piled up into a mound at the head end and it seemed to be a paler colour, glistening in the light of stars and fires. A heap of fresh branches and some logs were collected and placed beside the grave in readiness for the ceremony. Then we went back to where Jajjala lay, the people running with a high step round and round the little shelter, shouting 'Gah! Gah! Gah!' It sounded like the noise one often hears on the Nullarbor when the waves are rough out at sea and the air rushing along the limestone passageways suddenly escapes through a blow hole with an exhalation of breath, 'Gah! Gah! Gah!'

As is the custom we tied up the legs and thighs of the dead man, using the string I had brought with me because I knew it might be needed. We tied his left arm to the upper right arm, the hand resting against the chin, the right arm across the breast; he looked as peaceful as a sleeping child. The body was carried to the grave by four of his brothers and they lowered him down onto a soft bed of green acacia branches, my favourite tree, the tree that stands guard at the doorway of my tent stroking the canvas with thin trailing fingers. They covered him with more branches, green above him and green all around him because a Dingo man's body must not be allowed to come into contact with the earth of his grave. The branches were piled up until the hole was filled and logs were laid on the top and pressed down. Then more branches and the sand around was brushed smooth and level while the mound of sand at the head end was shaped into a half-circle. It made the grave look like a green bed with a smooth white pillow.

We went back to the camp and all through the night the people abandoned themselves to grief. I remember seeing the mother of the dead man and the sister of the mother of the dead man, lifting their faces and hands to the stars and crying out in their high voices so that the sound seemed to race into the heavens. They fell to the ground and beat at the hard sand with the flat of their hands. They ran together through the valleys of the sandhills and their echoing cries made me think of a pack of wild animals, hunting or being hunted in the night. All the others kept up the lamentation until the dawn: the deep murmur of the men, the high keening of the women.

A month later, on 22 August according to my notes, we performed the ceremony of laying the spirit of Jajjala. The men, the women and the children, each in accordance to their relationship with the dead man, lay with their naked bodies across the grave, and the women in particular performed this act in such a way that they seemed to embrace the grave like the body of a lover. Then the logs that lay across the body were lifted and set upright at the head of the grave, and the newly made hollow was filled in with more branches, and with decorated clubs.

I wish I could be buried like that when I die. I wish men and women and children would sit patiently around me during my final hours and when my heart had ceased to beat I would like them to dance round and round my dead body, Pah! Pah! Pah! Gah! Gah! Gah!, all of them crying in despair because Kabbarli had deserted them. I wish I could be wrapped in a nest of fresh green acacia branches and then I could feel the weight on my body as men, women and children lay above me under the stars and pressed themselves against me as a way of saying farewell.

They could bury me in the sand or they could place my body in a tree like that skeleton man I once saw who had been held inside a tree until the lightning came to release him. What a long time ago that was and I didn't have any way of understanding what it was all about although still it was a revelation to me, a mystery revealed. Yes, I would be happy to stand in a tree from one year to the next, or to lie in a hollow in the sand like a lizard waiting for a change in the weather.

· *Twenty-one* ·

Long ago when I was a child in Ireland there was a little village church that I would visit whenever I could. I went there on my own, secretly: in through the grey wooden gate, past the yew tree filled with darkness, along a gravel path that seemed to be trying to tell me something as I walked, under an archway, through a heavy door and inside.

Then I was surrounded by pillars of stone as tall as the trunks of huge trees; shafts of white and coloured light that fell like water from the high windows; a red strip of carpet poured out across the floor and up the steps leading to the altar; the glint of gold, or at least I think it must have been gold. As I stared at the high ceiling I could feel myself evaporating into the scented air and I felt that if I concentrated with all my strength I would have the power to do anything.

Over in a far corner there was a marble tomb with the carved figure of a woman lying on top of it like the decorated lid to a box. She was pale and beautiful with delicate naked shoulders, her hands folded across her breast and a baby wrapped in marble swaddling bands tucked under her feet. I stood close to her; touched the cold ruffle of lace, the cold hair, the cold skin. I stared at her as if into a mirror until she seemed to stare back at me through sleepy half-closed eyes. I never found out who she was or what she had done with her life before she let go of it; I don't even know how old she was when she died or what century she had belonged to. The expression on her face always seemed to be changing; one moment she looked quite happy, then sad, then so remote that you felt she had never had any interest in this world and certainly did not miss it now that it was gone. I used to think it would be nice to lie like that, white and beautiful for ever and ever and such a different sort of eternity to the one you might expect to find here.

This afternoon I was lying on my bed and staring at the moving silhouette of branches pressed against the canvas when I suddenly became aware of a young girl looking down at me. For a brief instant I felt as if I was that cold lady in the church somewhere in Ireland while the girl was me as a child, watching intensely and waiting for a miracle to take place. Then it was over and there was the fettler's daughter who had come to visit me, bringing a couple of letters and a custard cake her mother had baked for me.

The fettler's daughter has been coming here quite regularly ever since my last illness. She stands on the other side of the breakwind and calls out, 'Mrs Bates! Mrs Bates! Are you there, Mrs Bates?' Sometimes I invite her in and we have tea together. I suppose I must have been almost asleep and because I didn't answer she was worried by my silence and entered the tent to investigate. The fettler's daughter is about nine years old with a thin pale face, thin red hair, blue eyes. She might be pretty if she was a little more plump and if only she didn't look so restless and hungry, like a stray dog. She has the habit of putting all sorts of things into her mouth: buttons, spoons, stones, everything is smelt and licked and gently bitten. I have the skin of a red kangaroo on my bed, a very fine skin given to me by a man from the Pitjantjatjara tribe who they call King Billy, and the fur is soft and dense, fox red at its tips and grey inside when it is parted. As soon as the fettler's daughter saw it she fell upon it, rubbing her face into the fur as if she was searching for a nipple that would give her milk.

My tent is a palace of wonders for this little girl. One of her greatest pleasures is to examine the things I keep in the cloth pockets around my table. One day we took out all the mother-of-pearl buttons, arranged them in lines and counted them. I think she managed to swallow a button but I didn't mind, I have plenty. I have shown her how I load my revolver and I have taught her the simplest rules of needlework. She is quite skilled already, she mended a tear in my skirt when my eyes were bad and it was then that I shared one of my secrets with her; told her that I make all my clothes myself although people believe I have them made for me by the best tailors in Australia. She has promised not to betray me, not to anyone.

The fettler's daughter has no experience of anything beyond the life that is fixed to the Ooldea Siding; her days are marked by the arrival and departure of the trains, her years are measured by the heat and the wind and the distinctions that can be made between summer and winter. She has no brothers or sisters, no friends and although her parents are not unkind to her and have been very kind to me, they are always stretched to the limits of their energy and have little time for conversation or play. She says she is afraid of the low whites who scavenge along the line and I'm not surprised, they can be very frightening. She is also afraid of the blacks with their wild dazed faces and their dirty clothes, fascinated but afraid even though she knows they would never hurt her because she is my friend. But in spite of the smallness of her world she can understand so much. I tell her about Ireland where the hills are as green as the ones here are red, where the earth is as wet as this sand is dry and she smiles as if she is feeling soft rain soaking into her skin. I tell her about the fine houses I have seen and she is able to stand with me in the hallways, to walk along the corridors, to look out of the windows at the parklands that go on and on, further than the eye can see.

Sometimes I think that if Arnold had been a girl then things would have been much easier between us. I have shown the fettler's daughter the photographs I have of him when he was a child and she says how nice he looks, she would love to make friends with him. I wish I knew what has happened to Arnold. He hasn't written to me for years, or at least his letters have never reached me and I am no longer sure that I would recognise him if I did see him. There was that face in the carriage window of the train; but then why did the young man not wave to his own mother? Perhaps he did go to the War and then the Germans killed him; they would have been eager to kill him once they knew whose son he was. I imagine him lying in the mud in a field with no one to look after him in the way that I look after the people here who are dying; no Kabbarli to rub his poor body with oil, to comfort him and keep him warm by a fire.

Someone, I forget who, told me that Arnold is living in New Zealand, married to a woman called Lola, which sounds like a prostitute's name to me, and they have two children: a boy and a girl. If he has lost his memory because of what he experienced in the War then his wife must be very unhappy and I should help her. If I had a house, the lovely house I always meant to have, then the whole family could come and live with me and we would have such fun together. I would tell the little girl the Irish fairy stories that I was told when I was a child: the one about the man who became a wolf, the legend of Ballytowtas Castle, the story of the King of the Cats. And I'd tell her the Aboriginal stories as well, how Karrbiji brought water to Ooldea Soak in a skin bag; how all the land here was made in the beginning. I would teach her the names of the birds, the animals, the flowers, the stars in the sky. I would show her how to sew, how to mend broken bones, how to make cough syrup, how to make a concoction out of daisies that is so good for sore eyes.

I take the fettler's daughter on walks with me, when the weather is not too hot. Hand in hand we potter about over the red hills, exploring and talking. She thinks that I have magic powers because I can call to the birds and they answer me and sometimes a cloud of white cockatoos falls out of the sky and lands on me as if I was a tree laden with fruit. I teach her the English and the Aboriginal names for the things we see. Melga, the ground thrush; mirirl-yiril-yiri the wren and minning-minning his wife; burn-burn-boolala the bell bird; kogga-longo the white cockatoo; and kalli-jirr-jirr the black-breasted plover who leaves her eggs out in the open, protected only by their colouring.

The friendship started a few months ago when I was taken ill with pneumonia. My people were not with me, they had been driven away along the Line by the Germans and so I was very much on my own. Somehow the mother of the fettler's daughter found out that I was not well, I don't know how she found out but anyway she and her husband came to my tent with a stretcher and they carried me back to their house. She nursed me for three days and her little girl hovered around me, wide-eyed. I was so afraid of dying there in that tin house, it would not have been right at all. I had a high fever and apparently I kept repeating, 'Nardoo, nardoo,' which means no home, no home, not in the sense of a house but no homeland in which to be buried. I mustn't be ill again, or if it does happen I shall try to hide.

The fettler's daughter's father has made me a cool chest: a simple but efficient device that soaks up water from a bowl into a hessian cloth and keeps food a little cool for a little while. He also gave me a new empty potato tin for my shower; I suppose his daughter must have told him that the old one had rusted away. He is a handsome man and more gentle than most of the men you find along the Line; he gives food to the Aborigines when he has it to spare and his wife has a bottle of cough mixture which she makes with olive oil and lemon, especially for the derelicts; they do get terrible coughs that shake through their bodies. I did not know how to show my appreciation of their kindness after they had looked after me so I gave them a bottle of vintage champagne that I have had for years. I must be careful because if I seem to spend too much time with the whites then my people might think I have betrayed them and they won't come back to me.

The fettler's daughter asks me all sorts of questions. 'Why are you here?' she says. 'Why are you not living in a fine house in Ireland with servants and green trees and stairs as high as the sandhills at the Soak? And if you are here because of the blacks then why are they not here with you, where have they gone? And if you had a wish what would that wish be and if you had a second wish what would that be and if I was a lady in Ireland what would my bedroom look like?' I try to answer all her questions as well as I can. I explain that the Germans do not like me and they have driven my people away because they know that is the greatest cruelty they can inflict. I say that if I had my first wish I would go to Windunya Water up in the north and all my people would come with me and we would be a world within a world, far away from the Line, dancing the old dances, singing the old songs. Then the Government would appreciate my work and I would be made into the Chief Protector of the Aboriginals in South Australia and maybe the British Government would make me a Dame of the Empire and if I was a Catholic then the Pope would want to make me into a Saint, just as soon as I was dead and buried.

'But what if they refuse to come with you to Windunya Water?' the fettler's daughter says. 'What if they prefer to stay close to the Line, drinking and begging and watching the trains come and go?'

'Oh I think they would come with Kabbarli, if she had food, yes they would come, maybe fifty of them at first, then more later. But if they didn't then I would have Ratfin Hall.' I show her a pamphlet I have kept about Avon Castle which is very like Ratfin Hall in many ways and together we turn the pages, moving from the gardens into the house, exploring as we go. I tell her that all ladies sleep in feather beds, beds made out of white down as soft as ostrich feathers but softer and you must climb three steps to reach the bed, just like the three steps up to my observatory, but carved and polished. Then you lie in the bed and the flames from the log fire flicker on the ceiling, ancient wood sending you messages from long ago and a servant comes in with a hot drink and your husband comes in and looks at you with adoration. His face is the same as the faces of all his ancestors in all the portraits that line the walls of all the rooms. And when you die, I say, then your husband will miss you so much he'll have you carved in white marble; a life-sized figure of yourself, forever beautiful. And he will sit beside you and weep, because he misses you so much.

The fettler's daughter asks me why I have a cabbage stalk propped up against the trunk of the acacia tree that grows just outside the doorway of my tent. I explain that it is restful for my eyes; that my eyes are tired because they long to see the colour green again and this drought has lasted for so many years now, taking away all of the colours except for the blue of the sky and the red of the earth.

· *Twenty-two* ·

Today is as hot and quiet as yesterday. I never even heard the morning train going past; I wonder if it has broken down in this heat. What we really need is an earthquake or something else that would shatter the glassy sky and break the spell that has settled on Ooldea.

Ooldea seems to be in a sort of funnel, I can't think how else to explain it and I have no idea what causes it. Ten or twelve miles away they still have rain from time to time; not much but enough. Here there is nothing and there has been nothing for years. I have watched clouds approaching, big fat clouds bulging with the weight of water they are carrying, but as soon as they are directly overhead they begin to disintegrate. They stand very still with the wind pulling at them from all sides and then they are torn to pieces, dry limb from dry limb.

If a whirlwind comes into the funnel it stops spinning and the weight of sand that it carries at its centre is dropped down on us like a blanket. I rather enjoy whirlwinds although I know they can be dangerous. Once I had to cling to the ridge pole of my tent all through the night like a sailor clinging to the mast of a ship in a storm, but at the same time I was the storm, I was the spinning wind tearing at trees and stones, screaming in the darkness. The women say that whirlwinds thrust babies into their wombs and it is true that you feel you are held in a sort of embrace and you can't even hear yourself shout. After a storm like that the particles of dust can remain suspended in the air for hours or even days. The air becomes like muddy water and I have watched the moon and stars through a murky yellow haze that hung like a curtain before my eyes.

Quite recently we had a cyclone and that was very unpleasant; a cold wind raced in from the sea at Head of Bight where I was told an iceberg had been seen floating quite near to the cliffs. The wind tore at me for three days and three nights. It ripped holes in my tent and scattered my possessions in the sand. My hands were bleeding from trying to hold the canvas together while I stitched it.

My favourite wind is the tiny delicate one that comes suddenly out of nowhere and only lasts for a few minutes. Everything is quiet and expectant and then this cool breeze is caressing my face; it is as if a fan was being waved from another sphere, that is how I described it in my journal.

But the worst of all the winds must be the easterly sirocco. It goes on and on like a headache; it shrivels anything that has a scrap of green life in it; it pushes sand under my eyelids, sand into the melted butter, sand crawling between the sheets of my bed. It was a sirocco that killed my date palms. I planted several date stones in 1924 and much to my surprise two of them came up, green spears pointing at the sky. I watered them every day with my bathwater but they grew so fast I wanted to warn them to be more careful, this was not Arabia, they must learn to adapt. Just as I feared the feathery leaves became scorched and dry and they began to lose strength. Then the sirocco came and killed them.

On certain days I can wake up hungry for the colour green, aching with a desire to be among the hills of my childhood. When I was a child I was afraid of those soft hills that surrounded the place where I first lived, they seemed to me to be like a vast burial ground: people and potatoes, lying side by side under the earth. I used to think that perhaps there had been no hills before the famine, the land all flat and smooth until the dead came to put shape into it. I used to imagine a Last Judgement and everyone heaving up out of the wet grass and the mud; jostling together shoulder to shoulder. Sometimes if you stood on one of those quaking bogs you could feel it was about to happen at any moment; one crack and then another as the earth began to hatch.

I had a dream last night which was an Irish dream in a way. I was standing on a square of freshly dug earth about the size of a bedspread and lettuce plants started erupting out of the earth all around me, rather like those crabs on Bernier Island. Soon the black soil was covered by a dense carpet of lettuce heads and there was Sir Francis Newdegate standing on the edge of my garden, watching me. I picked some lettuces and gave them to him, 'You are a very wealthy woman, Mrs Bates,' he said, which was a nice thing to say. It makes me think of that lettuce I was given at the Beagle Bay Mission; one of the monks cooked it for me and presented it on a white tin plate so that it looked like something he had fished up out of the sea.

I would give anything for a drink of cold water instead of the warm liquid that simmers in the metal buckets and in my outside tank. My water is only fit for making tea and during the day the containers can be too hot to touch unless I wear gloves. The water at the Soak used to be sweet and cold, but that was long ago. When the mechanical heartbeat of the pumps stopped working it was so silent and empty there. I think that the end of the water supply from the Soak coincided with the beginning of the drought; the two went hand in hand or perhaps the one heralded the arrival of the other. I still go to the Soak occasionally to search for meteor stones, there are lots to be found there lying in the sand and looking like beads of black molten glass. The people call them sky-stones and value them highly and I always carry one in my pocket. I like to think of them as the seeds of other worlds, they do look very like seeds, so black and shiny and seeming to contain something within themselves.

I wonder if the ghosts of the dead have left the Soak now that the water has gone. I am sure there used to be thousands of them, a great silent army standing at the crossroads of the southern desert, watching and listening. Maybe they have all given up and gone away or they might have simply moved down to the Line to watch the trains; everyone else has. The people are mesmerised by the trains, the trains have become their life, the rhythm of their days. They set up their little shelters close to the track, modern shelters made out of sheets of corrugated iron or whatever else comes their way, and they sit and wait for the sound of that metal roar rushing towards them and then rushing away from them. Sometimes a gang of policemen arrives to break up their camps and then they scatter in all directions like a flock of birds, but they always come back, back to the Line. Whenever a train stops they run towards it; men, women and children staring up at the shining carriages.

I remember that old blind woman, Janjingu she was called and she had only just come in from the northern desert but she trotted off to the Line without a moment's hesitation. 'The new begging has been explained to me,' she said and she went and perched herself right on the edge of a wooden sleeper, standing firm in her own darkness and she didn't even flinch when she heard the train approaching. She held out her hands in a gesture of supplication and lifted her blind face upwards as if she was expecting God himself to reach down and kiss her. It was an act of faith and it worked. The train stopped right beside her although it had not yet reached the station and something about her appearance made everyone who saw her very generous. The windows of several carriages were opened and she was pelted with cooked meats, pieces of bread, fruit and cigarettes. She stood quite still until the inundation was over and then she peeled off the dress that I had given her that morning and piled her treasures into it, feeling for them on the ground. Naked and triumphant she set off back to my camp, never noticing the laughter that followed her.

Janjingu offered to share her food with me. The old people are always generous in that way, not like the new generation, the ones who have been brought up close to the Line and do not care for the things of the past. The young are wild and savage; they have no interest in the songs and stories of their ancestors, they are not controlled by the rules of their tribe and all they want to do is to float in the present moment, like rubbish pushed and pulled by the ebb and flow of a tide. They have no proper respect for me, these young cannibals, they forget that I am Kabbarli the white grandmother from the Dreamtime. I am sometimes afraid of them although I would never let them see my fear.

A few weeks ago there was great excitement at Ooldea and everyone is still talking about it, both my people and the whites who work at the Siding. A group of vaudeville artists were travelling on the train from Port Augusta to Perth and for some reason they decided to spend a night here with us. It certainly wasn't for the money, they seemed well-off and were travelling first-class and anyway the fettlers would never pay a penny for an entertainment, although they can be welcoming in their own way and will always provide food and shelter for a stranger. It can't have been for the pleasure of sightseeing either since there is nothing to see at the Siding and no one would want to try to explore the hills to the north in this heat. I think they were interested in seeing the Aborigines and they were glad to meet me as well. Then in the afternoon they put on a little entertainment just as a way of being friendly.

There were four of them, two men and two women and they called themselves by their surnames: Frankie, Heath, Osborne and Perryer. They were in the middle of a world tour that would take them well over a year to complete. They had already been to Africa, India and Thailand and once they had finished with Australia they had bookings in Wellington, New Zealand. I think that was their last stop before going home to England. They showed me a photograph of their names up in lights outside a very grand-looking theatre in London but although they were eager to talk about their adventures they were not at all boastful. I found them very attractive, so young and enthusiastic, and they said that I would have made a good actress, I have the right voice, a strong presence and lots of courage, courage is most important.

I met them quite by chance on the morning of their arrival. I wasn't planning to go to the Siding but then I thought I would look to see if I had any mail and I could collect some flour at the same time. The train was just pulling in as I arrived and a group of young Aborigines were staring at it with a sort of hungry expectation. Most of the passengers were gazing out of the windows and looking rather uneasy but suddenly one of the carriage doors was flung open and out leapt a young woman wearing a red checked dress that hardly reached her knees and a bright little saucepan of a hat. Her lips were painted as red as her dress which seemed all the more startling so early in the morning and when she saw me she waved as if I was an old family friend. I waved back, it was a long time since someone had given me such a friendly greeting. Soon the other three followed her, tumbling down onto the platform, all laughter and talk with the railway manager staring at them as if they were wilder than the wildest naked savage he had ever seen.

They began to take photographs of each other. One standing on the carriage steps waving enthusiastically at no one in particular; two standing arm in arm on the carriage steps; three clinging together and giggling as if they were circus clowns at a rehearsal. They asked me to photograph all four of them and that was how we started talking. They had never heard of me or my work which was disappointing but I didn't mind, particularly since they were new to Australia. They seemed to be very interested in the Aborigines and asked me all sorts of questions about them. They took a photograph of my friend Weejala sitting in the dust with her back to a broken table and one of King Billy, walking along the track with that look of sad nobility in his face, a digging stick in his hand. They wanted to photograph some of the younger ones but I couldn't help them there; a blonde half-caste girl with a baby on her hip ran away when they approached her as if the camera might be a gun and others stared with a sullen rage which was hard to look upon.

I would have liked to invite my friends to my camp but I explained that I must not allow white men to enter and they understood. We sat and talked in a patch of shade on the platform. They were amazed by how much hardship and difficulty I put up with. I told them how I have to carry every stick of wood for my fire, every bucket of water, every bag of flour. I told them how the station manager is in collusion with the Germans and so I have to pay extra freight charges for every item I buy from the train, while the fettlers get special cheap rates. My mail is tampered with and is often delayed for weeks. A list of vocabularies that I had sent to a friend in Adelaide was returned to me in tatters with fifty pages missing. I told them how important it was for my work to be published but the Government was against me and refused to help. A thousand pounds was all that I needed, all that I have ever needed; with a thousand pounds I could employ a typist and cover publication costs. They said it was shameful that a woman of my ability and determination should have been treated in this way. Your book must be published they said, it would be a crime if all that work was wasted.

They saw that I was tired and I went back to my camp to rest, having arranged to meet them again on the following day. As soon as I had gone the station manager wanted to ingratiate himself with them. He asked if they would like to put on a little show in the tin hut that goes by the name of the Ooldea Amusement Hall and they apparently agreed quite happily. So, on that same afternoon all the white residents came to watch my friends dance and sing; the fettler's daughter said that they were wonderful. A group of young male Aborigines had gathered outside the hall, attracted by the noise and excitement, and when the show was over someone had the idea of organising a tug-of-war between the blacks and the whites. I don't know quite what happened but the white team suddenly let go of the rope and the black team fell to the ground in a heap and then rushed off, angry and confused. The atmosphere at the Siding became very tense as the evening drew in and then some of the younger Aborigines took their revenge by defecating all over the floor of the hall, smearing excrement on the walls, the furniture, everywhere.

Understandably my friends were very upset by all of this. I suppose they must have felt partly responsible and they left on the early-morning train before I had a chance to see them again. Their visit made me realise how much I have cut myself off from my own kind, my own traditions. I don't for a moment regret the life that I have chosen to follow, but it is important to keep the bridge between the two worlds open. If I had seen them on that morning I think I might have asked if I could join them on their travels. I am sure they would have agreed; I am not an awkward companion. I so much wanted to tell them how glad I was that we had met, to say to them, 'You have been like rain to me, a shower of sweet rain in a parched land.'

· Twenty-three ·

The Station Master gave me a bundle of old Record Books. He said he was going to throw them away because they were out of date but then he realised they would be useful to me. Each double page is divided into several columns: one for the name of the Line, one for the name of the employee, one for the hours of work completed, the amount of money paid, the date, a signature. The paper is very thin so I can only use a pencil, but anyway it's difficult to use a pen in this heat, the ink dries too fast.

These little books are ideal for my vocabularies. There are still hundreds and hundreds of words that I have to write down because if I don't do it they will be gone for ever. I hate to think of words being lost like that, cut away from the things they are tied to, evaporating into silence. I hate to think that no one will know that this red sand has been called *munda*, while the moon slipping and sliding through the night sky above my tent is *beera*. The words can be as beautiful as a lullaby, even if you don't know their meaning or have forgotten which tribal group they come from.

I am also using the Record Books to make more lists of the names of the people who pass through Ooldea. I make these lists so I can inquire about the people later, find out what they are doing, if they are sick or in some kind of trouble. When I learn that someone has died I put 'dead' in brackets beside the name but I never cross out a name because I am sure that would bring bad luck. No one else has bothered to keep a record like this, little spider threads that connect the people together even when they are scattered. I have one book for the men and one for the women with their young children next to them on the same line if there is enough room. I also have a separate book for the younger women and the girls which shows their movements from place to place. In that way I can usually work out where their half-caste babies were conceived. If they were in one of the big prostitute areas like Tarcoola further west along the Line, then there is no way of knowing who the father might be, but in the smaller settlements it is easier. I hope this information will be useful to the Government at some later date.

When I am alone here and I am often alone here for months on end, then I read through the lists of the names of my friends until I have them all standing around me, my family. At the moment a few of the old and sick are camped quite near to my tent but the rest have all gone. I don't dare to feed my birds because an iguana has set up his home within the prickly safety of my breakwind and he would be quick to pounce on a little finch or a blue wren busy with crumbs and a drink of water. People and animals come and go, waxing and waning like the moon, only Kabbarli sits still. If I was stronger I might move on as well. I might say, 'Heart growing hot' and walk off north towards Windunya Waters, or even catch a train and go to Adelaide, stay in a nice hotel, talk to journalists about my life and adventures. But I cannot get out, I am trapped like Sterne's starling in its cage, or at least that's how it feels.

I did have a good supply of empty notebooks but now they are all filled up and I make my own diaries by stitching sheets of paper together. The paper bags they use for selling small quantities of flour are very good, so is the brown wrapping in which they send my weekly *Argos* newspaper. Other food wrappers are not so suitable since the mice are attracted to the smells and tastes they have absorbed. Someone gave me a pile of telegram forms but unfortunately the paper is too thin for stitching. It is important that I write something down every day, no matter how bad my eyes are or how weak I feel in my body. It doesn't have to be more than a few words, just enough to prove that one day has been different from another in certain of its aspects, otherwise it might seem as if one has no past or future, as if one lives within a twenty-four-hour circle, turning over and over in an endless repetition.

As well as keeping a journal I make notes on the backs of old envelopes or whatever else comes to hand. I keep notes and diaries in one trunk and manuscripts and vocabularies in another, but the heat and the wind make it difficult to organise these things properly. What I need is a cool office room with one entire wall honeycombed with pigeon-holes and then bit by bit I could separate out the tribes and the areas, the past from the present, my thoughts from the thoughts of others. I would have a ladder like they have in libraries and I would dart from pigeon-hole to pigeon-hole, labelling and cataloguing until it was all in perfect order.

The manuscript of my first book *The Native Tribes of Western Australia* could be ready for publication in a few weeks, it only needs retyping and editing. If I had a secretary and an office and a grant of perhaps ten thousand pounds then I could even produce a second book based on the work I have done here at Ooldea. The vocabularies and legends would be easy, and a number of my published articles from the *Australasian* could be included, but for the rest I would need time and money and no one could really help me. Here on this envelope for instance I have written, 'What they wanted they didn't know but they wanted something which only I knew they wanted.' From that I could write an entire chapter about Australia, mankind, the severing of time, the horrors of the past that are not extinct but are still with us now. On the inside of the same envelope I have written, 'They are starving, tragedy stalks before and behind them. Their food systems have gone. They are eating their own kind. The green strong rushes. The dead days of the afternoon.' That would provide me with the outline for a chapter about the Ooldea Soak, its history and the drought that has devastated it; the loss of traditional food animals that has led to cannibalism, the loss of the water at the bitter soak which once used to be hidden behind a curtain of green strong rushes. Perhaps it is dogs and not days, those thin hunting dogs that look as if they have stepped out of a medieval tapestry and the way they lie so still in the heat as if they were dead. Or it might be the deathly silence of the afternoons when everyone has gone away, or even the end of the day in a historical sense: the passing of the Aborigines. I am sure I could work it out if I felt stronger. Sometimes I have to write with my eyes closed because they hurt and then it is hard to read what I have written.

I have not been at all well recently. A return of the fever and I can feel the pieces of stone, grit and dust that have lodged themselves behind my eyeballs. I can count them piece by piece. I would think that a geologist could study the landscape I have seen from the desert particles I carry in my eyes.

This fever has been with me on and off for the last few weeks, ever since Christmas Day 1930 to be exact, when I had to fight with a bushfire that threatened to destroy all my papers. It's that which has left me so exhausted and has also made me aware of just how much work I have done over the years, how much valuable information I have collected. If it was all catalogued and placed in a library it would look very impressive.

The fire was nobody's fault. We had all been so hungry because of the drought, even the mallee bushes had turned brown and I only had enough money to buy flour and tea, I couldn't afford jam. The man they call Dhalberdiggin had chased a little lizard into a bush and when he tried to smoke it out the bush burst into flames which began striding across the land at a terrific speed. I saw it coming, a great bank of smoke on the horizon and I thought it was a rain cloud until I realised it was too low and the colour was all wrong. As the fire got closer I saw that the flames seemed to be eating their way across sand that was almost bare of any vegetation, as if the sand itself was burning. In the distance I could hear the fettlers down at the Siding shouting to each other and their voices sounded urgent and frightened. I suddenly realised that even the hills around my camp might not act as a firebreak and there was the danger that everything I owned would be lost.

My old people helped me; I think the father of the fettler's daughter came as well and together we hacked at the few straggling bushes and trees that grew around my breakwind until we had cleared an area some fifty yards wide all around. I had to be sure that my manuscripts would not be destroyed and so we dug a pit, it was just like digging a grave, six foot deep, eight foot long, five foot wide, enough room for a tall man wrapped in a blanket of leaves or for two metal trunks filled with papers.

Eventually the fire stopped only a few yards from my tent and a few yards from the edge of the Line close to the Siding. I would have been glad if the Entertainment Hall had been burnt to the ground, but never mind. The air smelt bitter for days afterwards and drifts of ash moved disconsolately in the wind. It seemed such a pity to have cut down what little vegetation had managed to hold on for so long. There was something absurd about the idea of a fire in a fiery desert, like rain falling into a lake or a fat man being given a hamper filled with food.

So then I was left with a fever that raged through my body just as the bushfire had raged through the desert. And one day I was lying in my bed when suddenly Radcliffe-Brown walked into my tent. He came in without even pausing at the entrance or saying something to warn me and he stood at the foot of my bed and stared at me. He was wearing round spectacles although I don't remember that he ever did, and they made his eyes glint in the dim hot light like a cat's eyes in the moonlight. His black cloak billowed out around him in the wind, it has been very windy again recently, and he had that gold-topped cane in his hand, the one he used to take with him everywhere.

He stared at me without a word and then he went over to the big table on which I have placed several piles of papers which I plan to sort through as soon as possible. I have two tables at the moment to help me with organising, but still I am short of space and I must get hold of another trunk from somewhere. The papers on the table are weighted down with flints – axeheads and cutting tools mostly, some that I have found myself, others that my friends have given to me over the years. I have a very fine collection, worthy of a museum, black and yellow and red flints, all of them made beautiful by the work that has been put into them. I love to hold a flint in my hand and to feel it absorbing the warmth of my skin.

Radcliffe-Brown picked up a flint and felt the sharpened edge with his thumb so that I could hear the sound of skin on stone as he flicked at it. Then he tossed it to the floor and goodness knows if I can ever find it again. He picked up the top page of the pile of papers that had been held down by the flint. It was a list of vocabularies beginning with some short sentences from the Central Australian dialects:

> I am angry
> I am not afraid of you
> Who are you afraid of?
> He is asleep.

He shook his head and muttered something so softly that I couldn't catch the words. He took a pencil out of his jacket pocket, and leaning heavily on the table that shook and trembled he began to write. He was crossing out my words, scribbling in the margins, underlining and still muttering to himself but more loudly now. I heard him say, 'No! No! No! No! This won't do! This won't do at all, Mrs Bates!'

I was very frightened but I summoned up all my courage. 'Put that manuscript down!' I said as if I was challenging a cat to let go of a bird that was still struggling in its mouth. 'Put it down at once! Now!' He turned and stared at me and he did look very like a cat with a bird in its mouth, the expression on his face blank and yet deadly. Then with one sweep of his hand he pushed all of my papers from the table to the floor, and he walked out.

· Twenty-four·

The fever made me feel so old: as old as I was, as old as I am. But then it passed and the rains came; or maybe the rains drove out the fever, I am no longer sure. I do remember watching those clouds as they approached and this time I knew that they could not avoid Ooldea nor could they carry the weight of their water beyond Ooldea. They were moving in from the sea at Head of Bight and they must have been hundreds of feet high. They looked like towering mountains of stone: grey, weather-worn slabs of granite that you could never expect to find here; glistening patches of snow, dark cracks where the rocks had broken away. Their contours never changed as they moved inexorably forward, pushing a whirling wind ahead of them that crept close to the ground and rushed around my feet like icy water.

Everything had been so silent because of the drought, but now the silence seemed to grow deeper and hold its breath in expectation. Then the world divided itself into darkness and light just as it did when I was with Jack and we saw the skeleton in the tree, but this time I was not afraid, standing there waiting and watching until the rain came clattering down around me. I tipped my head back so that I could feel it running over my naked face; I felt as if my skin was drinking, as if I was ripening until I could split open and step out of my discarded shell as young as I once was.

During the weeks that followed there were fresh showers every day. All the seeds that been lying dormant for so long uncurled themselves and erupted out of the sand. I was surrounded by a green lake in which all sorts of flowers began to appear; yellow on the mulga bushes, pink and blue in a sand that was now flesh-red and the extraordinary crimson and black petals of the desert sweet pea. Every day I would pick myself a bunch of flowers and my tent was filled with their scent. I was sorry that my date palms had not held on long enough; they would have enjoyed the rain.

Creatures I hadn't seen for years were suddenly with me again: a toad blinking and gulping, all my lizards but more shy than before, new birds, swarms of insects. And my people came back as well: old friends returning to see Kabbarli after having been away from her and new friends who had been able to complete the final lap of their journey now that the drought had broken. A young woman called Nabbari arrived at my tent after having walked more than a thousand miles from Mingana Waters beyond the borders of Western and South Australia. She was carrying her crippled son across her shoulders, just as I had once carried poor mad Dowie, and she was naked with bright red seeds fastened in the strands of her hair as if they had grown and ripened there. I would have liked to keep her with me, I would have liked to have gone with her, walking back the way she had come until we reached Mingana Waters, but she was impatient to go down to the Line and then I never saw her or her son again.

One morning I was called out of my tent very early; that soft buzzing cry of command I have heard so often before and three of my young men were on the hill that lies just behind my campsite. They were sitting beside the effigy of a snake that they had made out of dried grass in the traditional manner, but instead of it being covered with human hair as is the custom, they had used scraps of old clothes smeared with red and white clay from the Soak and a few white feathers that were probably stolen from a chicken at the Siding. The snake was about ten feet long and attached to a pole and as soon as I was with them they dug a hole in the sand so that it could stand upright and move in the wind. Then they produced a woman emblem made out of a motor tyre, also painted red and white with white feathers stuck to it. The car-tyre-woman was made to stand next to the snake-rag-man and they asked me to watch over them, to make sure that no one approached this place that was now sacred. It was nothing like the ceremonies I have seen before and shared in, but it made my heart leap all the same, as if this was a sign that we could go back to the old ways if we wanted to. I promised the men that I would keep their emblems safe and I took myself by surprise saying, 'When Kabbarli dies, bury her here. Kabbarli here, on this hill, looking this way back towards the red hills, not that way towards the Line.'

The rains made me realise how hungry I had been. I stood naked in my tent and with my dim eyes I stared at myself in the mirror. I could still see the narrow-waisted girl I once was, but I could also see an old white woman with empty belly and empty breasts. People would think I was a ghost if they saw me like that, a digging stick in my hand, walking against the tide away from the Line, back to Windunya Waters or some other deserted place filled with memories.

What I needed most urgently was money because I hadn't got any and I hadn't been able to write any more articles for the *Australasian* during the last stages of the drought. I thought of selling my totem boards to the Adelaide Museum but I couldn't send them by post because the maximum size of a package is three foot six inches and they were all at least nine feet long so that was not possible. I contacted my friend Professor Cleland, the pathologist at Adelaide, and he arranged for the University to buy my vocabularies for fifty pounds. It meant a lot of work copying out all those words from scraps of paper, envelopes and notebooks and my head ached with the task and with the curious sadness that came from sending the words away.

When the cheque arrived I decided to fatten myself up. I went down to the Siding four times a week to meet the passenger train and during the hour or so that it was waiting to have its tanks filled with water I sat in the dining car and ate and ate. I have watched how people gorge themselves after a long hunger and it was like that with me. I ate until my belly was tight and I felt my strength flooding back to me.

I always dressed smartly for the dining car and I met a number of very nice people. I got on so well with Lord and Lady Stanhope that I agreed to travel with them as far as Wynbring, about a hundred miles east along the Line. Once we had arrived I was able to catch the Tea and Sugar supply train back to Ooldea that same evening. Wynbring was a terrible place; flat, with dirty yellow sand, a few rough shacks near to the water tanks and no natives anywhere. I believe the police keep them out. I would go mad in a place like that.

Because I had money I could afford to improve my way of life. I arranged to have a little cart built for me in Port Augusta; just two strong metal wheels supporting a box with handles and room enough to carry more water and food than I could ever take on my shoulders. I called the cart The Augusta because that was where it was made and it was like having a companion come to live with me. It meant I could bring my flour sacks home in two trips instead of six and I could carry eight gallons of water at once. I had to be very careful crossing the pipeline which could easily damage my wheels; I tried to build a ramp, but the wind blew it away. I could never understand why The Augusta was much heavier when empty than when full, I wrote to the man who had made it to see if he knew but he had no answer for me.

While the weather was still so soft and fresh I had a letter from a book company asking if they could publish the articles I had written for the *Australasian*. I was going to agree until they said they wanted someone they called a 'trained anthropologist' to help me with the texts, and of course I couldn't accept such a suggestion and had to tell them so. Then, still in that same time which seems as far away from me now as a country across an ocean, a woman called Mrs Ernestine Hill arrived at Ooldea.

The fettler's daughter was talking to her when I went down to the Siding and she came and introduced herself, saying she had come here especially to see me. I knew she was a writer but I had not read any of her books.

Mrs Hill was a small woman: shorter than I am I would think and rather fat. She must have been less than half my age but she looked so strained and tense that I always had the impression I was younger than her. She was not very feminine either, or at least not according to my idea of femininity; smoked endless cigarettes which she said kept the flies away and wore trousers and a pith helmet like the one that Livingstone wore in the jungle. But she was very skilled at getting me to talk; said she had heard so much about me, wanted to interview me for the newspapers, learn about my wonderful life and help me establish my rightful place in history. She said that one day there would be a monument dedicated to my memory, here at Ooldea, and no one would ever forget Kabbarli.

I told her she could come and stay in my second tent if she didn't mind the discomfort and she said oh no, she was used to life in the bush, she had been to wilder places than this.

So for four or five days Mrs Hill was my guest. She didn't reveal much about herself except that she had a son called Bob who she seemed to have deserted and she was separated from her husband. She read out a list of the fifteen books she was planning to write and the thirty-six short stories, as well as newspaper articles, essays and plays, but for the moment she was going to concentrate all of her energies onto me. We would sit in the shade of the acacia tree during the day and by the fire in the evening and mostly I would do the talking while she listened and made notes in her notebooks. She had her own private shorthand which looked like a dreadful scribble to me, but then my eyes are very bad. 'Mrs Bates,' she kept on saying, 'you are a book. You are a whole shelf of books, filled with adventure and romance.'

I took her up the five rungs of the ladder that leads to my observatory so that she could see the stars, I showed her my cool chest and my shower made out of a potato tin. I showed her the metal tank in which I kept my manuscripts and the trunk containing all my personal papers. We examined the contents of the port-manteau case in which I kept my clothes and we counted my pairs of gloves; I even cut open the stitching on one of my calico bags so that she could admire my favourite pale grey suit.

Mrs Hill was fascinated by the story of my early life and I did enjoy telling her everything because it made it come alive again. I remembered that when both my parents died I was cared for by a woman called Mrs Goode who taught me how to do embroidery. I described the meeting with Queen Victoria in all its detail; what I had said to the Queen and what the Queen had said to me and the rapport that seemed to grow up between us. Then there was my work as an editor for Mr Stead on the *Review of Reviews* and my journalism for *The Times* which took me to Australia in 1900 or thereabouts. It was in Australia that I met my husband, dear Jack.

When Mrs Hill admired the kangaroo skin on my bed I told her about the tiger skin that had been given to me by an Indian Prince and how it had glowed with an inner fire. 'You have had many admirers, Mrs Bates,' she said, which is quite true. She was very curious to know how I have financed myself over the years, I think she has had quite a struggle herself, so I explained about the property I sold for £35,000 which became the foundation, the cornerstone, on which I built my work. She was very interested to learn that Radcliffe-Brown's present success is largely due to me since I provided the £2,000 to finance the Cambridge Expedition and worked with him as his assistant for two years during which I taught him everything I had learnt about Aboriginal society.

I could never be quite sure if Mrs Hill understood how important I am to my people; how closely we are connected so that our histories are intertwined. But no matter; scribble, scribble, scribble she went and she seemed very pleased with it all; said I was a miracle, a saint, the bravest woman she had ever met. But I was very tired by the end of the five days; the weather was suddenly as hot and as still as it had been before the rains and both my tables and even my bed were covered with piles of papers written in a handwriting that was not my own and that I was unable to read.

· Twenty-five ·

And then Annie Lock arrived at Ooldea. No, not straight away, she must have come in August 1933 while I was in Canberra. I was invited to attend a Government Conference there, to put forward my ideas about what should be done to save the Aborigines who were dying out; everyone knew they were dying out. I travelled first-class on the train; I was given a chauffeur-driven car and I stayed in the best hotels – all at government expense. I even managed to get to Melbourne where I rushed to see my friend Mr Hurst the editor of the *Australasian*. I found him sitting in his office under a very bright electric light bulb and I suppose I might have frightened him with all my talk and enthusiasm, but never mind.

The Conference was attended by a number of highly qualified individuals but none of them was able to under-stand the problems from the inside because none of them had lived with the Aborigines and learnt how to 'think black' in the way that I have. When it was my turn to speak I stood up in front of them all and I suddenly felt very inspired. I said that what my people needed more than anything else was land. The land was essential to them; it was what made them who they are and without it they are lost. They would need a big area, at least two hundred thousand square miles and perhaps more because it must be possible to walk far when you have to, when the 'heart gets hot' as they say. It would be desert land of course, dry, empty land that no one else would have any use for, but it must belong to them exclusively and no whites could enter without special permission. In that place there would be no need to wear the dirty clothes that make the people look like beggars and they would be controlled by their own laws and not by our rules and regulations which can seem so contradictory and cruel. Because no whites could enter there would be no alcohol and none of the new diseases, and with that I paused and stared carefully around the hall at the sea of faces turned towards me and I said, 'Do any of you realise what has been happening along the Line? How girls of ten years old or even younger are stolen from their families and raped and maltreated by gangs of white men and then thrown out like so much rubbish? Do you know how fast syphilis can take hold of a body and how it makes a person stink of decay? I have watched so many young men and young women come in from the desert shining and naked and then within such a short time I have buried them.' There was a low murmur from the audience, rather like a growl I thought, but I couldn't see much because my eyes were very bad on that day.

I said that the people could live in their own shelters; their shelters might look crude to us but they work well, they keep out the wind and let you watch the stars, the lovely stars and the moon moving across the sky. I said they would have their own dogs, they love their dogs and are heartbroken when the police come and shoot them. They could have as many dogs as they wanted and at night if it was cold their dogs could sleep around them for warmth. There should be a big fence, just like the dog fence near Wynbring, but this one would keep out the rabbits, the foxes and the wild cats that are destroying the animals that belong to the desert; to whom the desert belongs.

Then there would be enough food and people could hunt and live in the old way. If they got sick they could use their own medicines and it was amazing how well they knew the art of healing; I have cured all sorts of troubles just with the touch of my hands and I have seen how a fever can pass as soon as the will to recover has returned. I have also seen how people can die when there is nothing wrong with them except that they are sad and far from home. I know what it is like to endure extremes of heat and cold, of hunger, thirst and pain which no white person could ever tolerate. I have seen a man whose hand was smashed by a boulder hold it over a fire until he had burnt through the bone at the wrist and then he walked away, leaving the useless hand in the ashes just as a lizard leaves its tail in the jaws of an enemy.

I said, 'Ladies and gentlemen, I am a realist. I know that the past cannot be separated from the present for ever, but you must give us time to allow us to make the transition. I would suggest the appointment of a High Commissioner for Native Affairs, an English gentleman who could represent King and Empire and who would watch over my people from a distance and make sure that their rights were respected. I can think of a number of men of my acquaintance who would be ideally suited for such a job and I am sure that several of them must still be alive, I shall make inquiries at once. And of course I would be glad to help. I would give advice and guidance based on a lifetime of work that has brought me so close to these people that they call me Kabbarli, the grandmother. They would not object if I lived with them on their land and we would be too far away to cause trouble to any strangers. We could begin at once in an area north of Ooldea; I have always wanted to go further north where they say the sand is even more red. The hardship would not matter; I am accustomed to it by now; just so long as we had a source of fresh water and there are many hidden waterholes in the desert.

I said that everyone gathered here must understand that these people are children but they are good children in need of protection. 'If any of you lived close to the Line, as I have done for the last sixteen years, then you would know how dangerous the low whites can be and I am sure you would be horrified by their savagery and brutality just as I have been. I am so glad you invited me to speak to you because it restores my faith in justice and the British Empire; a faith which I must admit has been a little shaken recently. Now Kabbarli will look after her people like a shepherd with his flock and when they are ready she will open the doors for them so that those who want to enter the world of railway trains and big cities can do so, while the rest are free to stay.'

The hall was very silent and then the Chairman came and stood next to me and put his arm around my shoulder. He thanked me for coming to talk at the Conference and he said, 'I am sure everyone here will agree with me when I tell Mrs Bates that she is a quite remarkable woman; a brave, courageous, remarkable woman and we are all very proud of her. And is it really true, dear Mrs Bates,' he squeezed my shoulder rather hard when he said this, 'is it true that you are in your seventy-fifth year and yet you still look so young and, if you don't mind me saying so, you have such a pretty figure?' This question brought a rush of laughter from the audience and then everybody was clapping loudly and even cheering.

So that was it. I bowed and smiled and shook the Chairman by the hand but in the days that followed no one asked if they could discuss my proposals with me or even mentioned the fact that I had given a speech. And when I got back to Ooldea six weeks later, there was Annie Lock, guarding the gate of paradise. I think it must have been a plot; they knew they could never wade into my territory and steal from me while I was in my campsite so they did it during my absence. I sometimes wonder if I was sent the invitation to Canberra just to keep me out of Ooldea.

I could tell that something had changed as soon as I arrived at the station. People turned their faces from me as if they were ashamed and the fettler's daughter was nowhere to be seen although she had promised she would come and meet me. There was a lot of activity going on; crates and boxes being unloaded from the train and a horse and cart standing by the platform, ready to go somewhere.

I walked the familiar track to my campsite. I had left The Augusta at the station and now I used it to carry my luggage. The sun was very bright in spite of dark glasses and there at last was my tent behind its protective ring of brushwood, like an empty shell I thought. When I pulled back the flap of the door I felt as if I was an intruder entering someone else's abandoned home. It's funny how one's possessions can look so meaningless when they have been left on their own, as if the energy drains out of them when they are neglected. I found it hard to believe that I had lived in this little tent for so many years, slept on this rickety bed, kept my food here, my water there, my papers in that trunk and my clothes in this one. I picked up one of my favourite flints, a polished grey axehead, and I rubbed the smooth cold stone against my cheek, my lips, my tired eyelids. I picked up three little meteorites and scrunched them together in the palm of my hand so that they made a glassy scratching sound as if they were alive. I unpacked my suitcase, lit the campfire to boil some water and sat down with my back to the acacia tree. I suddenly felt as if everyone I knew in the world had died and I was the only survivor; a figure on a raft with the big ocean all around. I didn't cry, that came later, I just sat as still as I have sometimes seen my old people sitting; staring into a lost past; a tree remembering the forest that once encircled it.

Then there was a figure standing by the entrance of my breakwind calling to me softly. It was King Billy, my old friend King Billy, and he had his son with him but the child was hiding behind his legs. He had made me a present, a beautiful black walking stick that he had carved and polished while I was away, to show that he missed me. It was he who told me that Miss Lock had arrived and they were building tin houses next to the only water supply at the Soak and there was lots of food for everyone who came and said a prayer to Jesus and the police were rounding up the people, especially the children.

Later on that same day and on my own, always on my own, I walked as far as the hills that look down at the Soak. I stood like a frightened child, hiding behind the thin branches of a tree because I was afraid that if I was seen I might be caught by the police. My eyes seemed clearer although I did not want to see so much. There was the horse, waiting beside the cart, and I thought how often I had wished for a horse like that to help me carry my supplies. There were white men at work on all sorts of constructions: sheds and fences and something that looked as if it might become a chapel. There was hammering and shouting and I could see a group of my people standing in a huddle and watching a big white woman who was stirring the contents of an enormous cooking pot. The pot would contain a whole month's supply of my food and there must have been enough in it to feed every man, woman and child in the area. I could see sacks and boxes stacked around her in which there was more food for later. I watched as she picked up two white metal plates and beat them together like tuneless cymbals. Immediately there was a pause in all the noise and activity as if this was a familiar sign and then the big woman gave some word of command and out of the stillness came the sound of a church organ playing the tune of 'Onward Christian Soldiers' and a church choir began the words of the first verse in shaky gramophone voices. The woman joined in with a large and not at all shaky voice and then I realised that the people standing around her waiting to be fed were also singing. It was just like Radcliffe-Brown with Wagner under the flapping canvas, with the sound of the waves and all those flies, but it was much worse because at least then Tannhäuser and his triumphant choruses had been alone.

I went away before the music had ended and the food had been served and on the next morning, just as I had expected, Miss Lock came to see me. She stood at the entrance of my breakwind still wearing the apron from the day before, with her sleeves rolled up over her enormous forearms, her big broad face, her rancid Germanic smell.

'Ah Mrs Bates,' she said with a smile that looked very dangerous to me. 'Ah Mrs Bates, I have so much wanted to meet you and now here we are. I know all about the work you have been doing for the poor savages and I have such admiration for you, you have been an inspiration to me for many, many years. I do hope we can work together in helping our poor black brothers and sisters and bringing them closer to God.'

I didn't ask her to cross the boundary of my breakwind. I waited until her little speech was finished and then I handed her a letter that I had prepared in advance. In it I stated that there was no need for us to communicate verbally. If there was anything she wanted to know from me then she could ask me in writing. I would not be an obstacle to her work but I would be grateful if in return she could respect my need for privacy. That was all. When she had gone I cried like a child for the first time in I don't know how many years.

· *Twenty-six* ·

In the New Year's Honours List for 1934 I was awarded the Order of the Commander of the British Empire. I am still not quite sure what powers of authority this gives me apart from being able to write CBE after my name. I went to Government House in Adelaide to receive my medal and they pinned it onto the lapel of my grey suit: a little metal cross hanging from a pink and grey ribbon with a bow on it because I am a woman; the men do not have bows. I wonder what sort of metal it is, it gleams very beautifully, especially in the evening with the light from the setting sun. My name is inscribed on the back while on the front in the centre of the cross there is a double profile of King George and his wife Queen Mary. The King looks rather like my husband Jack before he shaved off his moustache.

I had always thought that Jack died not long after we saw that skeleton in a tree, I can even remember the funeral and how sad I was at losing him, but now someone has been telling me that he is an old man lying in a hospital on the west coast near Perth. Not that it makes much difference really, he will still float in my head in the same way, dead or alive. I used to see him quite often riding on horseback into the distance and I was always afraid that at any moment he might swing round and come galloping towards me, his teeth white under a big hat. He did frighten me, the way he clung to me so tight and sometimes in the morning there were bruises like shadows on my arms, my thighs, around my waist.

Only a few days ago I saw myself walking north across the sandhills and getting smaller and smaller. I know it couldn't have been anyone else but me, even though it is a strange idea and I think it must have been my Double; Mr Stead in London was a great believer in Doubles, he saw them all over the place. At first I was standing on the hill that lies just behind my campsite and I was staring at the tent and at myself sitting next to it. There was an expression of extreme longing on my face such as you sometimes see on the faces of the dingo dogs when they come prowling around and seem to be pleading with their eyes to be allowed to give up the wild and become tame. So there I was with my black stick and a white cotton coat that I often wear, but after our eyes had met I turned abruptly away and set off walking towards the north without ever pausing to look back. I must remember to ask King Billy if he saw me go, he sees everything that happens here.

I have been very upset by Miss Lock the Missionary. Everything about her is wrong: her body is too big and solid, her voice is too loud, the smell of her makes me want to sneeze. It is as if we belong to two different species and one of us is going to kill the other. She is completely illiterate; she wrote me a letter recently in her childish script in which she declared that all 'human beans' are equal in the eyes of God and then I had to laugh, seeing us lying side by side in a row a few inches under the soil, ready to sprout when the rain came. A row of beans next to a row of potatoes next to a row of graves and as a child I could never tell the difference between a potato patch and a burial ground, or so it seems now when I look back. In a way it would be rather nice to be a bean; white roots grasping the earth and those long green arms growing longer and longer, reaching for things to hold onto.

Yes, I have been upset by Miss Lock. I have done my best to avoid her and I have even told my people that they must go to her and not come to me, she will give them food and I have hardly any food; anyway if they don't obey her they will only be in trouble from the police. There are many of my people at the Soak now, more than two hundred I believe, and it's terrible to have them so close and yet not have them with me. I never minded before when they left me and I was alone because I knew that they would return, but this is different. Only King Billy comes from time to time to tell me the news, and the fettler's daughter.

They are building a dormitory down at the Soak and Miss Lock seems to want to make the children sleep there, under a roof and between the walls so that they can't see the sky. The police go around searching for the children who cry with fear and their parents try to hide them. I hid one child, a little boy called Archie – everyone has white names now, not black ones – I pushed him under my bed and told him to lie very still until the police had gone, but I can't keep him with me for ever.

Down at the Mission they have vegetable gardens within fenced-off areas where they grow lettuces, tomatoes, nice things like that, but it's easy for them because they can have as much water as they need. Miss Lock cuts the children's hair with a big pair of scissors and scrubs their skin with soap and water every day as if she wants to make them whiter. She likes the half-castes best because she says they are closer to God and I am told that she studies them with such a greedy eye it's as if she plans to eat them just as soon as they are fat enough. They are all afraid of her, I know they are. They sing hymns every day with the help of the gramophone and sometimes the sound is carried to me on the wind and it's as if I am standing there in one of those hot, airless, tin houses, dressed in rough cotton cloth that makes my skin hurt, stripped back to the bone with no one to protect me from Annie Lock, no one to look after me in the world except Annie Lock. 'The natives need a very firm hand,' she said in one of her letters and by that I'm sure she meant that she beats them when they disobey her, just as she beat poor Alice for eating a pomegranate she found in the sand. King Billy told me that no one was allowed to take their ration of food away and prepare it themselves, Miss Lock did all the cooking for them in her big pot and everyone stood in a line and sang hymns for their supper. The whole system of exchange has broken down because she never accepts any gifts of food in return, not in the way that I did when I was hungry and glad to eat a roasted lizard or the egg of a mallee hen. She is so fat she will never go hungry.

Things came to a crisis for me with the visit from the Duke of Gloucester in October 1934. I have always got on well with royalty, everyone knows that, and I still have the photograph somewhere in which you can see me shaking hands with Prince Edward when he was here all those many years ago. So the Duke was expected and I let it be known that I was ready to receive him and would be happy to arrange a display of native dances and skills, just like last time. In her reply Miss Lock said she thanked me for my offer but she was waiting for instructions from the Chief Protector and she would be in touch as soon as she knew what the plans were. So I waited because I had no choice and nothing happened, no word came to tell me what I was supposed to do.

The fettler's daughter was not sure when the royal train was due in and so I got myself ready very early in the morning and with my medal shimmering like a jewel I went to wait at the platform. There were many whites milling about, especially policemen, but I didn't see any of my people near the Line. I was told later that although they had been given new clothes in honour of the occasion it was not yet decided if they could be seen by the Duke and they were all made to stay close to the Mission.

The train pulled in at three fifteen and I sat very still and watched as the ladies and gentlemen stepped down with their top hats and fine dresses. Several of them smiled at me and a few gentlemen raised their hats, but I was waiting for the Duke. Then there he was, even more handsome than the Prince had been, and just like the Prince he got onto his horse and wheeled it around a few times before setting off at a canter, following the hard flat ground beside the track. He did turn to look at me before he set off.

The fettler's daughter said the day was a great success. The people were allowed to approach as far as the last line of sandhills and several members of the Royal Party took photographs of them. When the photographs are printed I will be noticed for my absence and I expect some questions will be asked. 'Where is Mrs Bates? Hasn't she only recently been awarded a medal by the King himself, surely she must be here somewhere?' they will say, taking a magnifying glass and scanning the black and white image, searching for me.

The Duke arrived back from his ride in time to watch a demonstration of boomerang-throwing although a wind was blowing so hard that the boomerangs did not return easily, or perhaps the people were not concentrating. I am sure the Duke was looking for me, wondering why I had not come to smile at him, never guessing that I was still sitting on a bench at the station. Miss Lock wanted to introduce King Billy to the Duke, probably because she knows that he is my good friend, and when King Billy would not bow everyone laughed although Miss Lock was rather angry.

Then the train began to whistle its loud urgent cry like some animal in distress and soon all the Royal Party was bustling back onto the platform. Before he climbed into his carriage the Duke paused when he saw me and he walked towards me, slowly, slowly so that I thought he would never reach me. We spoke for a short while as if we were old friends and then we shook hands and parted.

As I watched the train steaming and grunting out of Ooldea, I realised that I must leave as soon as possible. I wrote a letter to Miss Hill that same evening and I hoped that she could read it because my eyes were bad again and I could hardly see the glimmering whiteness of the paper. I said that I had reconsidered her suggestion that I should come to Adelaide so that she could help me to get my book ready. I would like an office and a secretary and I hoped that the *Advertiser* was still willing to pay me a good sum of money for the serialisation of my story, prior to its publication in book form.

Over the next weeks there was a lot that needed to be done and I wrote endless lists: the names of the people to whom I must say goodbye; all my possessions and where I had packed them or who I meant to give them to; all my notes and manuscripts and what subjects they dealt with; all my letters. I made a plan of the years from 1899 up until the present time because I was afraid I might forget something important once I had left this life behind me. I couldn't find any of Radcliffe-Brown's letters and I was sure I should have several of them so I hunted through a metal deed box in a state of panic as if the evidence that the past had existed was being stolen from me and there was nothing I could do to save it. Eventually I calmed myself by writing a description of the sky in the desert, how beautiful it is, how by looking at it one can feel as if one is sliding across the barrier and entering infinity.

Because I knew that Miss Lock disapproved of all the old ways I decided that I must hide the sacred totem boards that I still had in my possession. I oiled them one last time and then I dug a grave for them, lowering them down one by one as gently as if they were my own dead children. Then I scattered the sand smoothly all around so that no one would ever know what lay hidden there.

The fettler's daughter came to help me on the evening before my last day. I gave her the box in which I kept all my working tools: the needles and thread I used to mend the canvas of the tent, a little hammer, squares of leather for repairing shoes and boots, thimbles, string, pieces of cloth, balls of wool. I also gave her a couple of axes and a good spade but I kept my revolver, although I could see she would have liked that best of all.

I had sent a message to my people saying that Kabbarli was going away now, she had work to do in the city. They came early in the morning and I was woken by the familiar pattering of voices outside my tent, they even lit my campfire for me, just as they had done so often in the past. I gave them the clothes I would have no more use for: my gloves, my white cotton coats, my veils, my black skirts that had faded to a patchwork of dark greens. Birl, Jilyi and Kaarnga said they would help carry my luggage down to the Siding and off we went, with me leading the way pushing The Augusta.

So there I was again, on a platform, waiting for a train. The fettler's daughter came and sat next to me on one of my trunks and we sang a song together, one of the songs that I had taught her. A group of my people were standing close by and a woman I had not seen before, came up to me in the bright sunlight. She was carrying a naked sleeping baby in her arms and when I said how beautiful he looked she held him out for me to hold. I pressed his naked body against the beating of my heart so that he would not wake and for a moment I thought that perhaps I could take him away with me and bring him up as if he were my own child. Then I heard the noise of the approaching train and I handed him back to his mother, still sleeping.

Part Three

· Twenty-seven ·

MRS BATES ON THE RADIO

Daisy Bates is staying at the Adelphi Hotel in Adelaide. The year is 1936. She is seventy-six years old with another fifteen years of her life still to go. Although she will often struggle to return to the desert, scrabbling at a closed door like a wild animal in a cage, she will never be able to get closer than the edge; the edge of the possibility of return. And she will miss it. She will miss the bleak, hot, red hills of Ooldea as if it had been a paradise from which she was cast out; a place where she once knew a contentment she could not hope to find anywhere else.

A red desert now sits in her mind's eye and it is even more vivid than the green land of her childhood. She can see her little tent sheltered by its breakwind of thorn bushes and she can see herself: a white woman in a white tent. Crowds of black men, women and children have set up their camps close by. They are there all the time, they never leave her in spite of the drought and the hunger, in spite of the temptation of the roaring trains or the threats of missionaries and policemen. They come every morning before dawn to light her fire so she is woken by their soft voices. They sit through the days and nights talking to her; the old men give her their most sacred totems, they tell her the deepest secrets of their tribe; the women bring gifts of food and ask her to hold their new-born babies. She remembers how a naked woman with red berries woven into her hair smiles with relief when she reaches Kabbarli's camp at the end of a journey of over a thousand miles. All is well, the woman has reached her destination.

According to her own interpretation of the world as she knew it Daisy Bates had to come to Adelaide for a short time because she wanted to write a book about her work with the Aborigines, and also to sort out her anthropological papers. A secretary, an office and money-in-the-bank were waiting for her and this was a chance to complete her life's ambition.

On the day of her departure her people came down to the Siding with her. Many of them were wearing her clothes: the white overalls, the white shirts, the hats and ties she had offered to them as a parting gift. They stood on the platform with tears in their eyes as they watched her go, but they knew she would return as soon as possible because Ooldea was her only true home. And she knew that when she was very old these same people would sit close to her as she drifted towards death. They would be there to dig her a grave in the red sand, just as she had dug their graves, and they would call it a sacred place, telling their children the stories about the good white Grandmother from the Dreamtime.

But that is not what happened. Once Daisy Bates had left Ooldea there was no going back. And once she has left Ooldea I don't want to follow her movements too closely; instead I will try to catch a few glimpses of her, a small figure disappearing into the distance.

I begin with an excerpt from a radio interview. I cannot be sure of the date but I imagine that it was made in the late 1930s. I have listened to the recording and it is true that Mrs Bates had a remarkably soft voice, soft and clear with a slight Irish lilt. She is answering questions about her early life and being very vague and evasive. When the interviewer asks her how long she spent in a certain place she says, 'Oh I couldn't tell you anything about years because the one thing I can't remember is years. October 16th is my birthday, I can remember that.'

The interviewer wants to know more about her work with the Aborigines on the east coast, but for her the past cannot be disentangled, it is one rushing and tumbling stream in which everything happened at once and happens again before her eyes as soon as she turns to look at it. 'They died out so quickly and I have been watching them die out. Poor women, young women, girls, men and children, I saw them turn over on their sides and die, with their bodies still young, still fine, but the breath gone from them . . . I gathered up their legends, everything connected with them; data, yes, that's the word. Dialects. Every bit of it is straight, true. I got it from them, I saw it done. I would sit there at three o'clock in the morning drinking from my pannikin of tea, after the whole of the proceedings – getting all their dialogues, dialects, their marriage laws and so on and so on and their legends, you know . . . Perhaps I would have a cup of supper and sit there until four o'clock in the morning, when they went to sleep. I went in and sat down and I said, "Illi." "Illi" means name. I put it down straight off you see, and that was my way so I never got a word wrong. All my manuscripts are perfectly creditable and true. They loved to hear me say their own words in their own way . . . And I kept it up and kept it up. I never failed them, no, not for one hour of my time with them. I would go back tomorrow. That was my life. All the time among them was my life. I always wanted the whole of my life with them, all the time. I wanted to let the government know I didn't care a curse, a man's curse, I wanted through the whole of my life to be with them.'

· Twenty-eight ·

MRS BATES
AND THE TOMATOES

A man answered an advertisement in a newspaper asking
for information from anyone who had known Mrs Bates.
He had met her in Adelaide, it must have been in 1936.
He was turning down King William Street towards North
Terrace and there she was a few yards ahead of him. He recognised her at once, she was unmistakable although much
smaller and more delicately built than he had imagined. She
was quite a celebrity at the time, having only recently 'come
in' from the desert and there were articles in the newspapers
and interviews on the radio; everyone said she was a saint. It
was on the radio that he first heard her laugh; such a ripe,
wicked, unexpected laugh and not at all saintly. It made
him think of the joke about a mouse who drinks a bottle
of whisky and says, 'Now where's that bloody cat?'

A friend of his had been one of the party who went to the
station to welcome her when she arrived on the train from
Ooldea. He said it was extraordinary the way she stepped
out of the carriage like a queen and smiled at everyone who
was waiting for her as if her smile was a valuable gift to

each of her loyal subjects. Mrs Hill presented her with a beautiful bunch of flowers and she smiled at the flowers with the same benevolent intensity and buried her face in their scent. As they walked through the station hallway there was a boy selling bunches of violets and she stopped and gave him all her flowers, told him he must sell them and she hoped he would get a good price for them. Mrs Hill was very indignant but she kept silent.

They took her in a taxi to the Adelphi Hotel. The doorman in his uniform bowed a stiff greeting and she went up to him and stood very close, her face on a level with his chest, her eyes reaching for him. 'Would you mind if I take a bath?' she said. 'I haven't had a real bath for years, only a dip in a sawn-off kerosene can half filled with tepid water. I would so much like to sit in hot water right up to my neck and I shall soak and soak until at least fifty of my years have floated away and then you will be glad to see me young man, I'm sure you will.'

Nothing could stop her. The girl who came to clean her room in the morning was presented with a white linen handkerchief that had once belonged to King Edward VII and was told what a pleasure it had been to kiss the hand of Queen Victoria. In the restaurant she gave the waiter all the money in her purse, tipped it out into the palm of his hand because she said he had such kind eyes, just like the eyes of her son and her son's father. In a big department store she asked the shop assistant who was selling her some silk stockings, 'Do you know who I am?'

'Oh yes, madam, you are Mrs Daisy Bates.'

'That is quite right, but do you know that I am also Kabbarli, the spirit of the dead come back to the land of the living. You have no idea, no one has any idea, how much I loved my cannibals. I loved them more than I ever loved my family and that's a fact.'

So there she was now, scurrying ahead in front of the man who answered the advertisement, with her high-heeled boots and her long swishing skirt. She reminded him of the Red Queen, the one who says 'ouch' before she pricks her finger with a needle, and who grabs hold of Alice and rushes with her faster and faster so that she can reach the last square on the chessboard and escape from being only a pawn.

It was pouring with rain, soft, heavy, warm rain, but she had neither coat nor umbrella and her head was tilted back so that the rain could fall on her face. The pansies on her hat bobbed and waved and suddenly he saw a ripe tomato bounce down on the pavement in front of him. He picked it up and there was another and another and he realised that she was carrying a brown paper bag filled with them but the paper had disintegrated in one corner. He picked up two, three, four tomatoes and called out to her but she didn't hear. He followed her until they reached the steps of the *Advertiser* where she had her office and there she paused for long enough for the final tomato to fall and for him to catch up with her and introduce himself.

'Mrs Bates,' he said, 'you have dropped your tomatoes, the bag . . .'

'Isn't the rain lovely?' she replied, smiling as if they were old friends in the middle of a conversation. 'You know in the desert, the desert of Ooldea, I spent nine years without even a drop of rain. We were in a sort of funnel, I think that was the problem, and so the rain was sucked up at the moment when it might have fallen down. Aren't the tomatoes beautiful? I am going to eat them for my lunch. My favourite food is grated carrot with a spoonful of honey on top, but you mustn't tell anyone, it's a secret between you and me. Would you care to come to my office and meet my secretary, such a nice girl but I don't think I know your name.'

So he followed her up the stone stairs and into a little white office that can't have been much bigger than her tent in the desert, more of a cupboard than an office really, with three tables in it, one for the secretary, one for Mrs Bates and one for Mrs Hill. 'My amenuensis,' she said, pointing at Mrs Hill and winking at her new friend.

Both the secretary and Mrs Hill focused on Mrs Bates with a flurry of words and activity. She was told to sit in a chair while they pulled off her wet boots and her feet were rubbed dry with a white tablecloth. A radiator was drawn up close to her with her hat perched on top of it, steaming malevolently.

Mrs Bates didn't seem to mind all the attention although she was very rude to Mrs Hill. 'Mrs Hill is a writer,' she said to her new friend, 'and she would like to write my book for me but I have told her she can't because she has not had my experience of life and she does not understand any of the depths of human suffering. Anyway, she's not well and should be resting.'

It was true that Mrs Hill did not look well. Her face was tired and grey and her voice was a painful whisper. The man wondered if it was the work with this old lady that had exhausted her, drained her in some way. Still, they must have managed somehow because the book was written and it was a lovely book, very moving and passionate. It is difficult to know how much of it finally belonged to Mrs Bates and how much was the work of her amenuensis.

The man said he saw her again, one more time, or at least he thought he did. This was in the 1940s and he was on a bus and there she was running down a crowded street, the same grey suit, the same hat with the pansies, the same urgent, distracted enthusiasm. He so much wanted to talk to her again, there were so many questions he would have liked to ask her. He jumped off the bus as soon as he could and he ran and ran, pushing his way through the passers-by and looking for the familiar apparition. But he couldn't find her.

He went to the offices of the *Advertiser* and to *Woman's Weekly* and *Woman's Daily* and asked them if Mrs Bates was in town and where she might be staying. But they all said that as far as they knew she was not in Adelaide. They had heard that she had set up her camp at Pyap on the Murray River or that she had moved down somewhere on the south coast, Streaky Bay perhaps or was it Penong? The editor of the *Woman's Daily* said she had reason to believe that Mrs Bates was dead, but she had no clear idea from where she had got that information unless perhaps she had read about it in the newspapers.

· Twenty-nine ·

MRS BATES
AND THE POLICEMAN

There is an Aboriginal Reserve at Yalata. It's a few miles inland from Head of Bight where the limestone platform of the Nullarbor breaks off into the sea, but still some distance from the rolling red sands of Ooldea and the vast emptiness that lies beyond Ooldea. The land at Yalata is flat and peaceful, beautiful in its way with a thin forest of gum trees and low bushes. The sandy earth is a pale brownish grey. The people say, 'The earth here is the wrong colour; it makes us old; it turns our hair grey.'

During the 1950s and 1960s a number of nuclear tests were carried out in the deserts of South Australia. There are people who can remember the sound of those explosions that made the ground shudder and a terrible creeping black mist that seemed like the personification of all evil. The Ooldea Mission was closed down in 1952 and all the people who could be found in the area were herded together and made to leave. Some were taken in trains east to Port Augusta, west to Kalgoorli, others were sent on trucks to Yalata.

You approach Yalata along a rough dust track that branches off from the East–West Highway and when you get there you seem to be in a place that is caught up in a war, a famine, an epidemic, some disaster that is tearing it to pieces. Houses have their doors and windows broken and smashed and there are signs of recent fires. Cars lie helplessly on their backs among the rubbish and confusion. The people here look trapped, like refugees who have given up hope of ever going home; the expression on their faces is the same as the expression on the faces in those photographs I have kept for so long. It is as if they have been made to witness something unspeakable and they can never escape from it because it plays endlessly before their eyes, blocking out all other sight and sensation.

No one seems to be living in the houses but there are little camps set up among the trees; you stare and can distinguish one group and then another, camouflaged by insignificance. Over there is a piece of chicken wire with a blanket draped across it and there a sheet of corrugated iron propped up with a dead branch. There is a mattress on the bare earth with no shelter above it apart from the shade of a gum tree and there an open suitcase, its contents emerging tentatively like the soft body of a snail. Plastic canisters, portable radios, bottles, cars, dogs – but not as many dogs as I thought I would see.

I have come to meet Huwie Windlass. His father, King Billy, was a good friend to Mrs Bates at Ooldea and, although he was too young to remember much about her from that time, he also lived close to her in the early 1940s, when she set up camp at a place called Wynbring.

Wynbring was a station on the Line, a hundred miles east of Ooldea. It was a small unimportant railway siding where the big express trains never bothered to stop and post and food supplies were dropped off in the middle of the night, the train screaming in the darkness to announce its arrival. Daisy Bates was there between 1941 and 1945. This was her last campsite, the last time she was able to live close to the people she thought of as her family.

After Adelaide she had set up her tent at Pyap on the Murray River surrounded by green, tranquil farmlands, but that was no good at all with the Aborigines gone long ago and groups of tourists making special trips to come and see her, taking photographs and buzzing around her like flies even when she put up notices asking them to keep out and stay away. It was at Pyap that she made a bonfire in which she burnt a whole lot of papers relating to her past and afterwards she slowly made her way to Wynbring.

Her camp there was a mile from the Siding with two little tents surrounded by a dense breakwind which could protect her from strangers as well as from the weather. Table and chair, stretcher bed and metal boxes, a nail on the tree for the drying-up cloth, a metal tank for water, half a kerosene can for a bath and the other half dug into the sand to serve as a cool cupboard for vegetables when there were any vegetables. This was perhaps the most difficult stage of a stubborn and precarious existence: her boots broken and worn down at the heel and her eyesight too poor to mend them even if she still had her mending equipment; her calico skirts lined with the ragged remains of silk dresses to try and protect her skin which felt so delicate, as if a layer of it had been peeled away; a swollen toe that made walking difficult; a wound on the hand that refused to heal.

Dear Sirs,
    Will you kindly send me some pure lime-juice, however small the quantity, also, are there vitamins that I could take which would operate as milk, butter,

meat? I have tomatoes now and hope to get them
weekly and a few onions.

She had almost no contact with the whites, except a
fettler's wife who brought her the mail and a supply of
food, but many of the people who had known her at Ooldea
came to set up their camps close to hers. She tried to tend
the ones who were sick by rubbing their bodies with olive
oil and giving them sweetened lime juice to drink and she
was glad to talk to them about the old days when they had
all been so happy together. But many of the people were
much more wild and drunk than they had been before, as
she remembered them. They were like the low-whites now,
swearing and stealing and committing acts of violence. In
despair she banished them from her kingdom and for
almost two years she lived at Wynbring with only the
company of a few birds and a yellow iguana lurking in
the breakwind. At times she became very frightened, she
heard people creeping around her tent at night, tapping
out messages to each other, planning to murder her as
she slept, to take revenge. But she couldn't leave because
at least at Wynbring she was close to the edge of the red
desert, close to home. She must be patient and wait and
perhaps soon she would receive royalties from her book *The
Passing of the Aborigines* which was selling well in England
but had not yet been published in Australia. Once she had
enough money she could go back to Ooldea and inland to
Windunya Waters and then her people would be happy to
resume the old life and would forget about the trains and
the Line.

Huwie Windlass sits on a blue plastic canister, drinking
Coca-Cola and staring at me, assessing me. His wife lies
on the ground in the sun, her face on her arm, her arm in
the dust. A puppy lies close by, also in the full glare of the

sun. 'I don't come from here,' she says. 'I come from far, far away, Western Australia,' raising her arm and pointing with a finger as if she can see her own country somewhere beyond the blur of trees and bushes. Then she is silent and seems to be asleep.

Huwie Windlass begins to talk about the past; the pleasure of those days when you could jump on the trains and go far, far. The guards were angry sometimes, but you could climb on when they were not looking. The Missions were not so bad, he says, they gave you food and they couldn't stop you from leaving when you wanted to. 'We can't go anywhere now,' he says, 'and we can't live here, the earth here is the wrong colour. We can't live in houses, we need to see the moon moving, need to watch the moon and the stars, ah lovely, the stars,' and with a sweep of his hand he scatters the stars and the changing moon across the sky and admires them for their beauty.

'My father knew Miss Bates there at Ooldea. She was a good woman, eating our food, our bush food, talking our language, the Pitjantjatjara language. She keeps a fire burning as a sign she wants to help. She says you people mustn't drink, mustn't fight. You women stay away from the white-feller. No half-white babies here, only good black babies.

'She was at Wynbring, Miss Day Bates, old lady at Wynbring. One day the police come to our camp. They come with guns. They shoot at the people, pieouw, pieouw, pieouw, this way, that way, they shoot. They set fire to the blankets, you know the blankets they gave us, they burn them. They shoot the dogs, they shoot the water tanks, pieouw, pieouw. The people run, they are afraid. And look, here comes Miss Bates out of her tent, old lady with a gun in her hand. She points the gun at the police and she says, "You lot, you go away now!

You go away or I shoot you dead!" Then the police go.'

Huwie Windlass says she should have been buried at Ooldea. That was what she wanted and they should have done it for her, brought her back. He says, 'Have you seen Ooldea? The nice red sand? A big space, the high, high hills, but the sand moves in when the people have gone. Yalata is not my place. I belong Ooldea.'

A crowd of young men walk past, noisy and threatening. They seem like a hunting pack searching for something. An old man wearing an ancient, elegant yellow waistcoat with little mother-of-pearl buttons moves closer and sits down. He has a face of extreme sweetness, if that is a word that can describe a face. He smiles and then turns his head away shyly. 'Day Bates,' he says. 'Ah, Miss Bates, Day Bates.'

I try to imagine a little white lady in a long shabby skirt, eighty-five years old by now, emerging out of her tent and into the sunlight, brandishing a revolver and threatening to kill a group of policemen.

Before I leave Yalata, Huwie Windlass gives me a photograph of himself and two other tribal leaders sitting on some steps in front of the Houses of Parliament in London. He was in England quite recently as part of a deputation demanding the removal of the plutonium that has been left scattered across the desert not far inland from Ooldea. I have stuck this photograph into an album alongside pictures of the desert; the pale sand at the Soak; the East–West Line with a train roaring past in the evening light. Thin trees, vast skies, a few people in the distance.

· Thirty ·

MRS BATES
AND THE SWEET ORANGES

A fettler's wife who was living at Wynbring during the
1940s said that she could remember Mrs Bates quite well.
She arrived in March 1941 and was there until January
1945. No one had been warned that she was coming but all
her camp gear was sent on ahead by train: a pile of battered
trunks and boxes and a big canvas sack containing her tent;
each item addressed to Mrs Daisy Bates, For Collection,
Wynbring Siding, East–West Line. The Station Master
suggested they should leave it in the corner of an unused
shed until they received further instructions and then a few
days later the owner turned up in a taxi.

The fettler's wife watched Mrs Bates as she climbed out
of the taxi. She remembers her as being very tall and erect
which is odd when you consider that she was only five foot
two, but she must have given the impression of tallness.
She was dressed in a pale suit with a hat, a handbag and a
black umbrella and she looked as out of place as a creature
from another planet, standing there in a dusty street in the
bright sunshine, seeming not to notice the corrugated-iron

shacks, the piles of rubble, the dirty bleakness of this stop along the Line that existed only to provide passing trains with water. She stared out beyond the huddle of white people who had gathered around her as if she expected some friends to come rushing to meet her, come any minute now with laughter and shouts of welcome, taking her by the hand towards her real destination hidden somewhere out of ordinary sight. But no one came, the taxi driver left and the fettler's wife asked Mrs Bates if she would like a cup of tea, a rest after her long journey, something else that could perhaps be provided.

Mrs Bates answered with a vague private smile and said, 'I promised myself never to travel in a train, never again. Trains are such sad things, don't you think? I used to watch them come and go every day at Ooldea and yet I never got used to them. I have always wanted to fly in an airplane; up, up, up, until people look like ants and the land is a bedspread. That taxi was very uncomfortable, worse than a camel.'

The fettler's wife said, 'Are you planning to stop long with us, Mrs Bates?'

'With you? I won't be *with* any of you. My people will come as soon as they know I am here and then we will make plans. I will have my tent far from the Siding so I won't see you and you won't see me; I won't even hear your voices, or your radios if you have them on. But I can always walk in to collect anything I need and I've got my cart, The Augusta, so I can manage. If I do want help of any sort then of course I will pay for it. Right now I would like a few strong men to collect my belongings and then we can get the camp in order.'

A short while later the fettler's wife watched as Mrs Bates set off in a north-westerly direction, walking slowly but with great purpose across the pale flat land, with four men following her and one of them leading the Siding camel, loaded with her possessions.

She chose a site about a mile from the Line and she arranged for a thick enclosure of brushwood to be erected around her tent. Then she gave each man a shilling and turned her back on them as if they had already gone. 'Bloody old hag,' they said. 'Next thing she'll have a crowd of blacks clinging round her like flies. She'll be feeding them with war rations and digging graves for them, same as Ooldea.'

The fettler's wife said she hardly saw Mrs Bates for the first year. She was up there in her camp and four times a week she arrived early in the morning to collect her mail and whatever provisions she needed, tapping on a metal railing with a black umbrella to announce her presence and rarely prepared to exchange more than a stiff word of greeting. Once she bought a cake and once some scones and she did say she would be glad for some raisins or sultanas if the fettler's wife had any spare, but that was it. A group of about seventy or eighty Aborigines came in from the west and set up their little shelters close to her campsite and linesmen at the Siding blamed her for this invasion and wanted to stop her from encouraging them. They said she was turning the place into a squatters' camp and they even complained to the police but then all the Aborigines went again, as abruptly as they had come and Mrs Bates was on her own.

One morning very early the fettler's wife heard the rattling of the umbrella on the railing and there was Mrs Bates dressed all in black with black patches over both her eyes looking like a ghost that had lost its way. Her left hand and her wrist were bound in a crude bandage and her right hand was grasping the railing as if she might otherwise fall. As soon as she heard the familiar sound of the door opening she said, 'I am so sorry to trouble you. Pieces of sand from the desert lodged at the back of my eyes and now I can't see.

Can't get out and can't see, in a cleft stick you might say.'

The fettler's wife took her by one thin angular elbow and steered her into the house and towards a chair. 'Thank you. You are so kind, thank you. Please don't trouble yourself, I will pay you. Trouble is I can't see to cook and my hand won't heal even though I soak it in surgical spirit. I have never had any infection, not in all the years of dealing with disease, but I don't seem to be strong – lack of vitamins perhaps, no raisins, no milk and a lot of trouble with using war coupons. If you could make me one hot meal a day, I could collect it and pay you for it. You and your husband have been very kind, always.'

And so she came every day, walking as if in a dream across the land, pushing her cart ahead to steady herself and to act as a sort of guide dog warning her of any obstacles that might make her stumble. For a while she wore the black patches and then her face was hidden behind a thick veil. The fettler's wife thought that some of the linesmen left obstacles in her way on purpose and sometimes they would shout obscenities at her as she passed. One of them had a young black woman living with him and this woman hated Mrs Bates and would scream at her, 'Mamu, Bates, Mamu,' which means devil-creature or ghost.

It was her stubbornness that touched the fettler's wife. She couldn't like this old woman because she was so prickly and cold and even pity was difficult but she could respect her stubbornness. She saw how she dragged a railway sleeper back to her tent, working at it with the perseverance of an ant negotiating something five times its own size, and slowly slowly the heavy lump of wood edged its way from the Siding and towards her tent.

But then for five days Mrs Bates didn't turn up to collect her food or her mail and the fettler's wife decided that she must find out if anything was wrong. She was frightened when she reached the enclosure; it was as if the thicket of dead branches had grown up to protect the tent, like the wild roses around Sleeping Beauty's palace, but here it was old age that was being guarded, not youthfulness. She stepped through the narrow gap in the breakwind and everything looked so ancient and abandoned: an Irish linen dishcloth hanging threadbare from a nail on a tree as if it had been left there long ago by the swirling waters of a flood; a blackened saucepan perched on the cold ashes of a fire; a bundle of twigs tied together with string; a naked cabbage stalk; a broom to sweep away all this grey dust.

The door of the tent was open and the fettler's wife walked in. She didn't call out because by now she was convinced that Mrs Bates was dead and cold and so there was no point trying to disturb her. She needed to accustom herself to the dim light, the canvas heat, the musty smell of old age and something sharp that was perhaps vinegar or the fumes of surgical spirits. Then she realised that Mrs Bates was sitting on the bed, dressed in the remains of a white silk nightdress, as still and upright as a buddha with one leg stretched out in front of her on the sheet and the other bent with the naked foot in her lap. She was rubbing and pinching at the big toe and she was so preoccupied that she never saw her guest standing there.

The fettler's wife felt as if she had entered someone else's dream and maybe that was why Mrs Bates did not notice her. She looked around at the clothes scattered on the floor, silk stockings, old-fashioned undergarments, a blue satin dress that seemed to have been cut in two just under the bodice, shoes with broken heels. There were piles of paper everywhere, on the floor, on the table, on the chair, the bed. A tin bowl filled with old tea-leaves was on the bed beside the old woman, a bottle of lime juice stood so close to the edge of the table that it would surely fall and there was a bowl of what must have been beetroot balanced on some papers on the chair; that was probably the cause of the acid smell.

The fettler's wife went away, quietly stepping out of the canvas cave, out of the charmed circle of the breakwind, down the dirt track and back to the Siding. Afterwards when her heart had stopped racing she wondered if Mrs Bates had indeed been dead. Was it possible to sit upright like that when there was no life? Maybe she had died a few minutes before and the body had not yet registered the change?

But no, a few days later there is the familiar tapping of the umbrella on the railings and there is Mrs Bates, looking much better. 'Did you wonder where I was?' she asks, almost coyly. 'I had trouble with my foot, dropped the corner of a wooden sleeper onto my big toe, couldn't fit into any shoes, not even riding boots, and didn't want to walk to the Siding with slippers because people would laugh. I had some supplies; a lovely cabbage and a beetroot which I cooked myself. When I couldn't sleep I watched the stars and thought of the Yalata legend about how the stars were made. I must write a book of those legends when my eyes are better. They are improving, I have been bathing them with tea-leaves and the toe is not so bad. Oh, I almost forgot, my son came to see me, wasn't that nice? He came to my tent and stood there smiling so kindly. Did I tell you about my son? His name is William. He fought in the last war and now he is on his way to fight in this war. That was why he came, to say goodbye to his mother.'

The fettler's wife says, 'How nice for you Mrs Bates. A letter came for you today as well. I can read it aloud if your eyes are still a trouble.' The letter is from the Governor of Western Australia. He is going to be passing through Wynbring on his way to Perth and he would so like to stop to say hello, it must be twenty years since they last met.

'Well,' says Mrs Bates. 'A distinguished visitor! Would you mind coming to my tent tomorrow morning and then you could be my mirror. I must be presentable but I might miss the finer details. I can show you my little home and we can take tea.'

And so the fettler's wife goes for a second time to the tent within its breakwind and she spends an hour or more helping Mrs Bates to look her best. They unstitch a calico bag and pull out a pale suit like a new skin. She helps with the lacing, the tying and the buttoning and then together they walk down to the Siding. That evening Mrs Bates eats supper with the fettler and his wife in their little corrugated-iron house and all three of them are tense with the expectation of the sound of the approaching train. The train is due to arrive at eight o'clock, but it doesn't come and doesn't come and finally just before midnight they hear it in the distance. Then the fettler and his wife run the two hundred yards down to the Siding, almost carrying Mrs Bates between them. They stand there together by the big water tanks – there is no platform at Wynbring – and Mrs Bates laughs with excitement as the big express steams towards them, its brakes squealing. The Governor of Western Australia puts his head out of a carriage window and waves a greeting to Mrs Bates and the fettler lifts her up as light as a bird and places her into the open carriage door, where the Governor grasps her by the hand and she disappears. Ten minutes later she reappears, laughing in the darkness. 'Look,' she says, 'I have been given some oranges. Catch!' and she throws three big oranges one after the other for the fettler's wife to catch and wrap into her skirts while the fettler lifts her from the high step and they set off back into the night.

'The oranges are for you,' she says. 'I don't care for oranges much, but the Governor tells me that they are very sweet.'

She walks home to her tent in the dark with a little torch and the fettler and his wife eat two of the oranges before they go to bed. They say they have never tasted anything as sweet.

The fettler's wife doesn't remember much happening over the next couple of years, but towards the end of 1944 a new group of Aborigines arrived to set up their shelters close to Mrs Bates and that seemed to make her very happy, although she hardly spoke to the white people now. On Christmas Day 1944 the fettler's wife prepared a meal for her and took it to her tent. She came to the edge of the breakwind to receive the tin of food and said proudly, 'Look, they have come back. My children, the children of my people at Ooldea. They call themselves the Kabbarli mob and we are making such plans together.'

The fettler's wife is not sure what happened next. Some people said that Mrs Bates became very ill and needed help, others thought that the authorities wanted to get her out of the way and break up her Kabbarli mob. An ambulance car arrived one morning in January 1945, with a driver, a nurse and a policewoman. When they tried to persuade her to come with them she shouted and screamed like a wild animal and even when she was in the car she fought so hard that she managed to open the door and fell out onto the dirt road.

Not long after she had gone a group of policemen came to collect her tent and all of her belongings and they set fire to the little shelters that had been erected close by. The fettler's wife thought that Mrs Bates had died shortly after they got her to hospital in Port Augusta, but that was only a rumour.

· *Thirty-one* ·

MRS BATES
RUNS AWAY

Mrs Bates said she had nightmares for months afterwards; she had never been treated like that, her body bruised all over, and she would wake up struggling and shouting for help, tearing at the hands that held her down while the ambulance car jolted and lurched over the corrugated surface of the road from Wynbring to Port Augusta. In her dreams the hands of the policeman and the nurse seemed to burn into her flesh like an acid, even where her skin was covered by the protection of clothes. The smell of them had frightened her as well and that also made its way into the dreams: a sweet cloying smell so that she suddenly understood exactly what the old people had meant when they said 'the smell of the white man is killing us'.

She said they took her to a hospital in Port Augusta and she has no idea of how long she was there, weeks maybe, or months. The nurses were kind but they treated her like a child, a little orphaned foreign child, and there were bars on all the windows. She wanted to get her strength back so that she could return to her people, but she knew it would be unwise to mention her plans. She also wanted to find out what had happened to the papers she had kept in a metal trunk in her tent at Wynbring. She could remember seeing it standing open in front of her while she put more papers into it: handfuls of them from the bed, the table, the chair, the floor, until the trunk was filled to the brim. She could remember closing the lid and taking the key to lock it, but there her memory stopped dead, the key seemed to fall from her hand and the next thing she knew she was in the car, fighting for her life. Nobody at the hospital was willing to tell her where the trunk might be or what had been done with the key. The more questions she asked the more they smiled at her, blank meaningless smiles as if her language was not theirs.

After Port Augusta she was moved to a hospital in Adelaide where she was free to go out whenever she wanted to. But the city had changed almost beyond recognition. People shouted at each other and often she couldn't understand what they were saying because their accents were so unfamiliar. She wondered if it was the War that had done it; brought in a new sort of wildness. She was frightened by the close presence of the buildings, the crowds of hurrying strangers, the confusion of the traffic. Sometimes she lost courage when she was in the middle of crossing a road, standing there wide-eyed until someone came to steer her back towards safety. Once she was knocked down by a passing tram, but she was not badly hurt, just shaken.

She said her brain felt so heavy and dark, as if it was bruised just as her body had been. She thought she could find some sort of quiet again if only she could walk in the wind but there was no wind in Adelaide, hardly any stars. Then one morning very early she decided to leave the hospital, walking out without telling anyone where she was going and with only the clothes she was wearing and a handbag. After three days of staying in cheap hotels, each one worse than the next, she heard about a bus, the Bird's Eye Bus it was called, that made a regular journey from Adelaide to Streaky Bay, down on the south coast and not too far from Head of Bight. So she bought a single ticket from a woman whose name really was Mrs Bird's Eye and sat herself down in the deep leather seat of a sky-blue car that called itself a bus.

It was over four hundred miles from Adelaide to Streaky Bay and all the roads were dust tracks riddled with pot-holes and the ridges formed by the rush of floodwaters. But Mrs Bates clung to her handbag and clung to the knowledge that she was on her way towards home. She had heard that some of her old people were in the region of Fowler's Bay, about a hundred miles west along the coast and they would soon know that she had arrived and was waiting for them.

She said that she liked Streaky Bay from the first moment she saw it: the quiet shallow sea streaked with seaweed and banks of dried seaweed along the shoreline as soft as a feather bed. Pelicans drifted by, studying their own reflections in the water and pink parrots gathered in noisy crowds on the rooftops and the branches of trees just before sunset. People here were busy with their own lives and not much interested in each other or in a stranger like herself.

The two hotels at Streaky Bay both belonged to the Mudge family. Mrs Bates took a room at the Criterion which was run by Miss Mudge and was cheaper than the Flinders Hotel run by Mr Mudge. She said she had a very nice room with a washbasin and a fly netting over the window. A black cat called Tiddles used to come and stare at her through the netting but she never described the view from the window; whether she looked into an enclosed back yard or down the street and across to the wide horizon of the sea.

The hotel had no staircase but still she managed to get lost along the single corridor, looking for her own room and walking into rooms that were not hers. One of the resident guests was a Mrs Miller, who was eighty-five years old, the same age as Mrs Bates. I imagine the two of them accidentally confronting each other in the corridor and for a moment wondering if a full-length mirror had been set up to block their way.

Mrs Bates also got lost in the few streets of Streaky Bay. She said she kept on finding herself in someone else's back yard surrounded by heaps of junk cars – jeeps they are called, or is it japs? Anyway it would be nice if she could make herself a little tin house from all this shining metal, with the roof, the floor and the door in different bright colours.

Streaky Bay had once belonged to the Kookata tribe, a tall handsome people if you judge them by the few photographs that have survived, but they had all gone long ago except for one old woman who was called Annie Wombat. She wandered back and forth through the town and slept on the dried seaweed by the beach or under a tree or in someone's garden. Everyone tolerated her and laughed at her and said she smelt like a dead fish but Mrs Bates never mentioned Annie Wombat in the letters she sent to friends.

Mrs Bates used to leave the hotel quite early in the morning and then she would walk all through the day and return just before dusk. Her papers had still not been traced but she had enough money to live on and a suitcase of her old clothes. She used to go out with the black walking stick made for her by her friend King Billy and she had a little axe strapped around her waist, hidden by the flap of her long jacket. The policeman at Wynbring had confiscated the revolver and it had never been returned, but the axe made her feel safe. She walked along the sea-shore, even in the rain, collecting shells and the little fossilised wasp nests that you can still occasionally find lying among the pebbles beyond the reach of the usual tides. They look like white stone cocoons and must have been made out of some pale clay long ago; the people call them Angel Boots. Sometimes she would build herself a fire out of pieces of driftwood, staring back towards Ooldea and hoping that her friends would see the thin line of smoke in the sky and would know who it must come from.

Then one day she heard news that old Gooyama and Ngarri had been seen further along the coast. She set off at once in a taxi to the next town of Ceduna and there she booked into a hotel and started work: wandering through the streets, asking shopkeepers and passers-by if they could provide her with information. Whenever she saw a group of black derelicts sitting in the dust on the side of the road she would go up to them and say, 'Kabbarli, Kabbarli,' waiting for the magic of her own name to produce a shout of recognition. One of the shopkeepers seemed to be very friendly and eager to help and so Mrs Bates gave her a cheque and said, 'If they come, my two old people, Gooyama and Ngarri or anyone else who knows me, then please give them food: bread, tea, sugar, meat if there is enough. Just say the word *Kabbarli* and they will understand.'

From Ceduna she hired another taxi to take her further along the coast to Penong and Bookabie, but there was no one there either and the taxi driver went home. She managed to persuade Mrs Wiess, the wife of a German shopkeeper, to drive the final stage of her journey down to Fowler's Bay. They went across the thin glistening surface of a salt lake where a cloud of white birds flew just ahead of them as if showing the direction they must take. They drove alongside the white sandhills separating the land from the sea, shining almost pink under a blue sky and everywhere there was a stillness that was not quite desolation. Mrs Bates sat in the passenger seat, searching the land with her almost blind eyes for a sign of human movement, pulling with all her strength towards her people wherever they might be.

They stopped briefly at Fowler's Bay and then went on towards Koorabie. There, just before they reached a rough settlement of houses she saw them: four or five old men and old women sitting in the dust. The car stopped and Mrs Bates wound down the window and called to them, 'Kabbarli, Kabbarli.' They did know her then and they rushed around the car so that Mrs Wiess was terrified by the wildness of it all: the dirt, the matted hair, the eyes, the teeth.

And now I can seem to see Mrs Bates, dressed in a white suit and stepping out of the car and into the bright sunlight. Three old men and two old women stand around her eager and smiling, but distant, terribly distant. But she is happy and feels as if she has achieved her aim, she has come home.

And that was it. They spoke for a while and exchanged news about who was still living and who was dead and then they parted. There was nothing more that could be done. That evening in the Ceduna Hotel Mrs Bates wrote the first of many letters to the Minister of the Interior in Adelaide. She said that this was an emergency. She must have a horse and a caravan sent to her at once, immediately. She must have food and medical supplies. As soon as everything was ready she would be setting out towards Yuria Waters with the friends she had already contacted and any others who wanted to join her. The sand there was not as red as it was at Ooldea but she had been told that there was fresh water at all times of the year and they would be out of the way of any intruders.

· Thirty-two ·

MRS BATES
AND THE ISLAND SHIP

At Streaky Bay I walked over the soft banks of dried seaweed along the shoreline, searching for shells and those little fossilised nests that are called Angel Boots. I watched the pelicans gliding past on the smooth water, the cormorants sitting with hunched wings at the end of a disused jetty, the pink parrots quarrelling softly in the branches of an avenue of trees.

The Bird's Eye Bus that had brought Mrs Bates here in December 1945 was sitting in a shed in the courtyard of the town museum, next to an enormous threshing machine with red painted sides. I peered in through an opened window at the steering wheel anchored by dusty cobwebs and the deep leather seats that looked as though they would never willingly relinquish a passenger.

Inside the museum that had once been a school I looked at early radios and washing machines, clocks from the 1920s and mirrors from the 1930s, home-made chairs and tables, patented butter churns and three-wheeled bicycles. On a bookcase facing me there was a collection of glass jars and bottles, each one containing a small reptile, insect or fish native to this area, floating in a preserving fluid. Some of the containers had lost most of their fluid so that the creatures they displayed had become strangely amphibious, half dried in the air, half soaked in the liquid.

In one of the classrooms there was an elegant glass cabinet in which you could see Mrs Bates's black walking stick that had been made for her by King Billy, her little axe, a copy of *The Passing of the Aborigines*, a lavender bag, a few photographs, an envelope labelled 'seeds from my garden' and a birthday book with a passage from Shakespeare for each day of the year. The owner of the museum opened the lid of the cabinet with a screwdriver and when I looked through the book, searching for familiar names, I saw that the day on which Arnold Bates was born had been carefully torn out. She had marked her own birthday in pencil: 16 October, 'Daisy M. Bates, age 88, 1948.' The identical cabinet next to this one contained photographs of the last members of the Kookata tribe and a few of their decorated wooden implements. A shark's jaw was hung on the wall alongside a blue crab with spidery legs, a few native spears and a coloured print which I seem to remember was showing the state funeral of Queen Victoria.

In the other classroom there was a big double bed, a child's cot and a dressing table on which had been placed a brush and comb and a few little pots made out of pink plastic. An elaborate satin wedding dress was fitted onto a tailor's dummy and a wall cupboard was filled with all sorts of clothes including Mrs Bates's pale beige gaberdine coat, beautifully mended at the cuff and along the edge of the pockets. One button was a different colour to the others and the front was stitched to the back through the button holes, so I could not ask if I could try the coat on.

The owner of the museum took me to meet a woman

called Mrs Thompson who had lived in a remote farmhouse several miles east of Streaky Bay during the 1940s, with Mrs Bates staying as a paying guest for more than a year. She must have moved to the farm immediately after the hunt for her friends along the coast. Maybe it was cheaper and she was short of money, or she might have felt the need to be further away from too much human company. Mrs Thompson said she was never any trouble, used to make her own tea in the mornings, and must have washed her own clothes although there was never a sign of them hanging out to dry. She went walking every day even when it rained, setting off in a south and easterly direction and staying out until the evening except when she had visitors, but that was not often.

Mrs Thompson sat at a round table with the curtains drawn to keep out the heat of the day and she showed me photographs of herself and her family with Mrs Bates as they all had been almost fifty years ago. 'She was a funny old fish,' she said, 'as cunning as a native. Very old by then but there was nothing wrong with her, she had her own common sense. We had a maiden aunt staying as well, a rather proper sort of person who liked to tell the kids how to behave. Daisy used to sit next to her at the table and she would wink at the children and nudge them with her foot to make them laugh while the aunt was lecturing them. She loved playing with children, singing songs and dancing as if she was a child herself, but she was always much nicer to one of my daughters and that stirred things up between the two of them and made trouble.

'I remember when Jack Orn, the man who rode all the way round Australia on a bicycle, came to see her. He was a fine-looking man with a big red beard as wide as a spade and she sparkled like a young girl, showed him how she could swing on the children's swing, how she could touch her toes and skip. I used to hear her skipping in her room every morning. Twenty times quite fast, she said she had always done it, even in the desert when it was too hot to move.

'For a while she brought me a cup of tea early in the morning, which was nice of her although she used to leave the cup by the open door so I had to get up anyway. Then there was a time when my husband was not at home for a week or more and a male cousin came to stay. On his first morning with us she marched into his bedroom without knocking on the door, flung open the curtains and stripped the covers from him where he lay sleeping, as naked as a baby. We didn't speak about it afterwards but I never got another cup of tea from her in all the months that followed.

'We used to worry when she didn't come back before dark. Once my husband found her out in the fields and not so far from the house, busy digging herself a hole in the sandy earth to sleep in, just like the natives do. He picked her up in his arms and carried her home; she was so small and thin it was easy to lift her. Another time when there was no sign of her he went searching and searching everywhere. She had gone down the narrow coast path that leads to the sea from High Cliff, facing that steep rocky island that we call The Granites. He said he saw her standing there in the moonlight, soaked to the skin and as wet as a shag, and she was calling to the island. She thought it was a ship, a ship in full sail; it does look a bit like that at times, especially in the moonlight. I suppose she thought she was marooned somewhere and needed rescuing, or perhaps the ship was going to take her back to Ireland where she came from. My husband had to sling her over his shoulder in a fireman's lift so he could steady himself with his hands going up the path and I can remember him coming in with her clutching him around the neck, smiling like a new bride. She didn't say anything but she gave me a wet hug and I led her into her room and helped her peel off the top layer of her clothes, which was difficult with all those buttons and hooks to be undone. She looked so frail in her silk petticoats, a bird without its feathers, and when I tucked her into bed she pulled the sheet right over her head and still said nothing.

'She showed me all her clothes one day, very proud. "This one, I wore to the Duke of Gloucester's wedding; this one I wore when I met the King of England." She was so tiny she could still fit into all those old things and they were beautifully made, some of them. She said she could only have silk next to her skin, anything else burnt her like an acid. Her eyes were not good, because of the sandy blight I suppose, and I helped her with mending and made her a pair of crêpe de Chine knickers which she was very pleased with.

'She never spoke to me about the natives, although there was a young man who once came to visit, and they sat together in her room for hours. When he left he told me she had shown him a suitcase filled with native vocabularies and stories, and he thought they really should be kept safe in a library. She wanted him to take all these papers away and make them into a book, but he was not qualified to do something like that. Then that woman Ernestine Hill arrived, and I think she took a lot of papers away with her when she left. I know Daisy was not happy about it, I heard her weeping in her room. It's a pity her son William never came to see her, she told me he was living somewhere in New Zealand but he had suffered a great deal in the last war.

'She left us in October 1948, and when she went she gave me all sorts of things I didn't know what to do with; I kept them for a while and then passed them on to the museum. I still have a set of negatives and photographs she gave me. There are some of her in the desert with a camel and a buggy piled high with luggage and a couple of natives, a man and a woman, both of them smiling. It looks to me as if they are in the sandhills up behind Eucla somewhere. At least that would be my guess because I know she was once in that area. She gave me a signed copy of her book *The Passing of the Aborigines*, and I remember she said, "I wouldn't read it if I were you. It's not much good." '

· *Thirty-three* ·

MRS BATES
AT OOLDEA

After she had left Streaky Bay Mrs Bates went to that house
on the outskirts of Adelaide where Douglas Glass came to
visit her in 1948; where he made photographs of her skipping in the garden, looking at the pages of a book with
the light from a window shining through her white hair,
holding the stems of three daisies and staring at them with
an expression of unexpected tenderness. Then she was in a
hospital for a final year until her death on 18 April 1951.
She was buried in Adelaide Cemetery and it is said that a
hundred people attended her funeral, but there were no
Aborigines among them. A metal plaque commemorating
her work was fixed to a brick wall at Pyap on the Murray
River, and a little memorial was erected on the edge of the
railway line at Ooldea.

And so here am I, standing in my own memory beside
the railway line at Ooldea. It has rained quite recently, not
heavy rain but enough to intensify the redness of the sand,
making it look as if you could slice it through with a knife,
like bread. The sand is pitted with tiny volcano mounds

made by the ant-lions that Grant Watson used to collect in their many varieties on Bernier Island. The leaves of the mulga bushes are a soft sage green, and some of the bushes are decorated with yellow flowers and caterpillars masquerading as flowers. I have since been told that if you clap your hands to a rhythm the caterpillars will nod their heads to accompany you, but I didn't know that then. Other plants are erupting out of the ground and if I were patient enough perhaps I could feel their vegetable movement pushing against the palm of my hand.

There is only a rough track leading to Ooldea from the main East–West Highway, and you must have a guide to make sure that you keep to it and realise when you have arrived. There is no station here now, no platform, no buildings, no noticeboard to tell you where you are; nothing that makes this into a place at all except for the strange memorial to Mrs Bates, looking like a post box that has lost its human purpose and has been left stranded in this enormous landscape. The train track cuts through in a straight line east towards Wynbring, west towards the Nullarbor, and when a train is approaching from the distance everything seems to hold its breath and tremble in anticipation of the sudden scream of racing metal wheels.

The memorial is painted white and it stands close to the Line, waiting there patiently, watching the trains come and go. A metal plaque is fixed to it on which there is the image of Mrs Bates looking rather sinister with her round spectacles like the eyes of an insect, and King Billy, naked with a long beard, holding what must be a sacred totem board. The two figures are separated by the inscription: '1860–1951. Daisy Bates devoted her life here and elsewhere to the welfare of the Australian Aboriginals.'

There is a lot of rubbish near to the railway line. A pile of concrete which I suppose might have been part of the station platform, several wrecked and rusting cars, broken wooden sleepers and concrete sleepers, lengths of piping, sheets of corrugated iron, empty tins and empty bottles. I am surprised by the quantity of old clothes that lie scattered across the ground: knitted jumpers, torn skirts and blouses, the remains of blue jeans, the remains of shoes. Everything is bleached and battered as if it has been left out in a succession of wild storms. Things cling to the sharp branches of the bushes or lie in stiff heaps. I see something which at first I think is a fragment of someone's bright pink silk dress, but then I realise it is only one of those little parrots whose colour has not faded with death. There are lots of rabbit skeletons as well, and big white bones that must have come from cattle or horses or even the camels that once used to work here.

I walk a little distance away from the Line until the soft waves of the sandhills surround me like a vast red ocean. It would be so easy to get lost; all the bushes and all the hills look the same and nothing stands out as a landmark to steer you back to where you have come from. The quiet is suddenly enormous.

That evening, the sound of the flies scattering their feet on the metal roof of the camping van in which I am lying makes me think for a moment that it must be raining. The sun sets very abruptly, trailing red streaks across a black and purple sky and then the bats come out, calling to each other in the darkness. I think two or three trains go rushing past during the night, but the noise merges with my own dreams which I have forgotten when I wake. I remember the cool air of the dawn flowing across my face like water, and then the unfamiliar electric calls of birds whose names I did not know.

I have arranged to meet a group of old people who were all at Ooldea during Mrs Bates's time and who are now sometimes to be found at a makeshift camp further along the Line, close to a station called Watson. They arrive in two trucks while it is still early in the morning and I watch them clambering down: old people in old clothes. I walk towards them and some seem not to see me while others smile shyly. I am introduced to a woman called Nellie Queama with white hair cut short in a stiff fringe, grey-dark skin, paper-soft delicate hands, toenails as sharp as the claws of a hunting dog. She reminds me of my old friend Edith Young, the same defiant expression, the same sudden intimate laughter, a peppery human smell, but maybe I exaggerate the sense of familiarity so as to feel less isolated among strangers.

Nellie Queama had known Mrs Bates. 'Oh yes,' she says. 'Miss Bates here,' staring around as if she expects a veiled woman in a long skirt to walk towards us from out of the sandhills at any moment. I ask if she liked Mrs Bates and she says, 'Oh yes, good woman. She gives us clothes,' patting the blue T-shirt she is wearing, the old skirt.

I shake hands with a woman called May who has also known Mrs Bates, but she is less approachable, her shyness heightened by the sandy blight that has attacked both her eyes and blinded one of them. The two women have a dog called Tricker; a big thin hunting dog like the kind that used to be carved in stone and made to lie under the feet of dead sleeping gentlemen in village churches; a quiet watchful dog that waits to be told what is going to happen next.

And here comes the man I had seen at Yalata with the yellow waistcoat, the mother-of-pearl buttons and the curious sweetness of expression. And a few others, old men and old women, friendly in their way, but inhabiting a world that I can only see from a great distance and cannot hope to enter.

We pile into the back of one of the trucks among ropes, water containers and petrol cans. I sit between Nellie with her dog and the man in the yellow waistcoat who stares fixedly at the passing landscape and sings as we judder our way towards what remains of Mrs Bates's campsite.

Then we stop, and here we are on one round sandhill that looks the same as all the others, with a view down towards the Line and a view back into the desert. The people busy themselves with examining the ground, as if they are looking for evidence to prove what they already know. 'Daisy here,' they say. 'Daisy she sits here and she looks this way, ah, yes. She sits and she looks that way, ah yes, very nice.' They show me a smudge of ashes and burnt wood that they say is where she had her campfire, and they point to the thin rings of rusted metal that are the remains of the kerosene cans that held her tent down, and stopped it from flapping away like some great bird when the wind blew in from Head of Bight. I find a mother-of-pearl button, and someone hands me a lead post office seal with Port Augusta stamped on it. I am also given a gun cartridge, a metal hook-and-eye fastener which might have belonged to a pair of high boots, and a thin elegant bottle which I like to think has once contained lime juice.

It seems such an odd place to choose as a campsite, there is so little flat ground, so little shelter. But maybe the sand has moved and changed its shape during the years that have passed since she left. Presumably someone has cut down the acacia tree that used to stroke the canvas of her tent at night and against which she propped the stalk of a cabbage so that her eyes could rest on something green when the desert seemed to be dead for lack of rain.

I walk with Nellie and her friend May up a little hill that looks down on the campsite. Nellie keeps smelling the air, saying how nice it smells because of the rain, how fresh the sand, how green the trees, but when she is not smiling her face has a look of terrible sadness. I ask her to tell me the names of things: that round bush, that bird, that tree, suddenly understanding how a vocabulary could seem to hold the secret of a people, as if the words were thin threads that could somehow connect you to a different way of seeing and explaining what can be seen.

After an hour or so we leave the campsite which was a home for Mrs Bates for sixteen years, and we set off towards the Ooldea Soak. The truck rushes through the soft sand, pushing past the branches of trees that trail like curtains in our way, until we have reached another place that also looks like no place at all.

The Ooldea Soak is an area of flat pale sand surrounded by red hills that used to be much higher than they are now. Tufts of luminous bright grass show where water can still be found close beneath the surface, and one of the old men digs a hole in the sand so that a pool of water seeps up, cool and sweet-tasting. All that is left of the pumping machinery is a few broken and rusty pipes, and all that is left of the mission house, the church and the dormitories is a few sheets of corrugated iron. One of the old men picks a small pomegranate from the tree which used to stand next to the dormitory where he slept when he was a child. 'Thou shalt not steal!' he says, laughing.

You feel as if you are in a vast amphitheatre here, with the hills all around like the tiered seats for an audience. It is not difficult to believe that you are being watched by an unseen crowd of hundreds and thousands of men and women, perhaps even birds and animals. There is a sense of expectation, as if with a shout of command the land will crack open and a stream of living things will tumble out of it, stretch and stare about.

The pale sand under my feet at the Ooldea Soak is

covered with fragments of bone, tiny scatterings of bone, most of them no bigger than grains of wheat. There are also flints, black and yellow, red and grey, all of them cut from the quarries down by the sea and brought here at some point in the past, maybe many thousands of years ago, or quite recently and just before the mechanical heartbeat of the pumps was set in motion. Before we leave the Soak we sit for a while in the hanging shade of a pepper tree, and Nellie gives my daughter a triangle of flat red stone that has a hole cut into one corner and geometric lines scratched across its surface. She gives me a meteorite she has just found, a densely black dome-shaped pebble, like a drop of molten glass, and it is easy to see why the people call them sky-stones. I have it here now on the window ledge in front of me where I am working, I like to think of it as the seed of another world.

· Select Bibliography ·

Because Daisy Bates gave contradictory accounts of her life and work I have had to steer my own path through the information that is available. Wherever possible I have used letters and diaries, rather than published material, as my source, but although I have kept close to my understanding of the facts of Daisy Bates's life I do realise that this book is a very personal interpretation and for that I take responsibility.

The largest collection of Bates papers is held in the National Library of Australia, Canberra. They have fifty-two boxes of notebooks, photographs, etc., including the Eucla and Ooldea notebooks, which I found most fascinating. They also have Elizabeth Salter's biographical papers which include the transcript from a radio interview and numerous letters from people who had known Mrs Bates and responded to a request for information that was published in the Australian newspapers during the late 1960s.

Letters, papers, magazine and newspaper articles, photographs etc. relating to Daisy Bates are also held in the Australian Institute of Aboriginal and Torres Strait Islanders Studies, Canberra; the Battye Library, Perth; the Barr-Smith Library, Adelaide; the La Trobe Library, Melbourne (which holds the complete Hurst correspondence from 1918–46); the Mitchell Library, Sydney (with documents relating to Morant and Bates); the Mortlock Library, Adelaide (with the most interesting letters from Wynbring and Streaky Bay); the State Records Office of South Australia, Adelaide (with letters from the missionary,

Annie Lock and information relating to Wynbring and the establishment of a mission at Ooldea.)

Bates, Daisy, *The Passing of the Aborigines*, London: John Murray, 1938, second edition with foreword by Alan Moorehead, 1966

Berndt, Ronald and Catherine, *From Black to White in South Australia*, Melbourne: Cheshire, 1951

Bolam, A. G., *Trans-Australian Wonderland*, Melbourne: 1923

Brady, M., *Leaving the Spinifex: the impact of Rations, Missions and the Atomic Tests on the Southern Pitjantjatjara*, Records of the South Australian Museum, vol. 20, May 1987

Burke, David, *Road Through the Wilderness. The Story of the Transcontinental Railway*, New South Wales University Press, 1991

Denton, Kit, *Closed File* (the story of Breaker Morant), Adelaide: Rigby, 1983

Gara, Tom, with Sally Brockwell, Scott Cane and Sarah Colley, *The Archaeology of Daisy Bates' Campsite at Ooldea, South Australia*, Australian Archaeology, No. 28, 1989

— with Scott Cane, *Environmental, Anthropological and Archaeological Background to the Nullarbor Plains*, Anutech PTY Ltd, South Australia Heritage Branch, Nullarbor Plains Project Stage 1, January 1988

Hill, Ernestine, *Kabbarli. A personal memoir of Daisy Bates*, Sydney: Angus and Robertson, 1973

Mattingley, Christopher, ed., *Survival in Our Own Land*, Adelaide: 1988

Moorehead, Alan, *The Fatal Impact. An account of the Invasion of the South Pacific*, London: Hamish Hamilton, 1966

Salter, Elizabeth, *Daisy Bates. The Great White Queen of the Never Never*, Sydney: Angus and Robertson, 1971

Whitcome, Eleanor, *From Sainthood to Scandal. The murky legend of the mysterious Daisy Bates*, The Weekend Australian, 2–3 April 1988

White, Isobel, ed., *Daisy Bates. The Native Tribes of Western Australia*, Canberra: National Library of Australia, 1985

Watson, E. L. Grant, *But to What Purpose?*, London: Cresset Press, 1946

— *Journey Under the Southern Stars*, Abelard-Schuman, 1961

— *Where Bonds are Loosed*, London: Duckworth, 1914